CfE Higher PHYSICAL EDUCATION COURSE NOTES

CfE Higher PHYSICAL EDUCATION COURSE NOTES

Caroline Duncan • Linda McLean

1 Introduction

When studying Higher Physical Education, you will learn about your own performance and how it can be improved. The process you go through will involve reflecting on what you already know from your study of PE, from the other subjects you have covered as part of your National Qualifications and from the work you completed as you worked through your broad general education (BGE).

In this book you will learn more about the **factors that impact your performance** (FIP) and you will be given practical approaches that you can apply in order to develop your **performance**.

The structure of the Higher course

The Higher course is broken down into two internal units:

- Performance skills
- Factors impacting on performance (FIP).

The **course assessment** consists of:

- A single performance – a special or one-off event
- An exam which will be based on the four factors – **mental, emotional, social, and physical.**

Exam 40 %
Performance 60 %

The single performance is worth 60 marks or 60% of your final mark.

The exam is worth 40 marks or 40% of your final mark.

Performance skills unit

You will probably cover different activities in the Higher course. From these you will choose your two strongest activities and try to achieve a pass overall for these two activities.

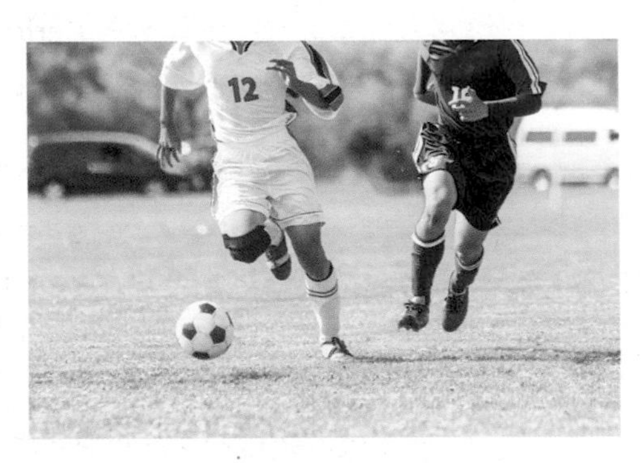

Within the performance skills unit you will have to consider the following outcomes and assessment standards:

Demonstrate a broad and comprehensive range of movement and performance skills in physical activities by:

- Selecting and applying a broad and comprehensive range of complex movement skills, displaying a high level of control and fluency.
- Demonstrating precise body and spatial awareness with distinct patterns and rhythms.
- Working cooperatively with others.
- Using well-established techniques, composition or tactics.
- Making appropriate decisions in challenging contexts.
- Reacting appropriately and making effective, safe adaptations in response to a wide range of challenging variables.

Factors impacting on performance (FIP) unit

In this unit you will look at the impact of **mental, emotional, social** and **physical (MESP)** factors on your performance. You will consider how to gather information on your strengths and weaknesses, how to develop your performance and, finally, you will have an opportunity to monitor and evaluate your performance. The approaches you use will encourage you to think more deeply about **why** you carry out this process and to reflect on changes you might make based on your progress and the results you obtain as you try to develop your performance.

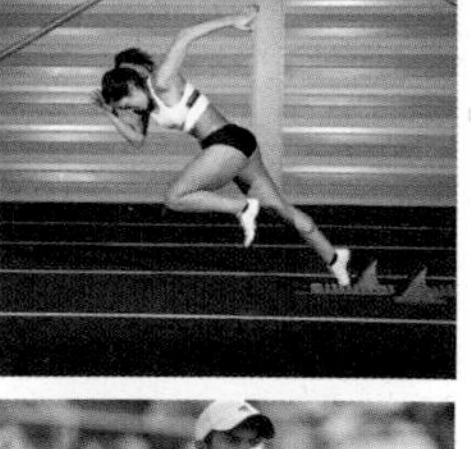

This book gives examples of the types of tasks you can use to help you complete this process and to gain a good understanding about how you can apply your knowledge and skills in different activities or performance situations.

Within the FIP unit you will have to consider the following outcomes and assessment standards:

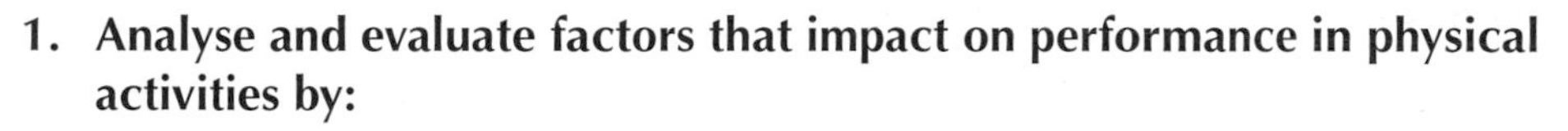

1. **Analyse and evaluate factors that impact on performance in physical activities by:**
   - Analysing methods used to identify factors impacting on a performance.
   - Evaluating the impact of positive and negative factors on a performance.
   - Explaining approaches to performance development based on these evaluations.
2. **Evaluate the process of personal performance development by:**
   - Producing a personal development plan that sets appropriate development targets.
   - Selecting methods to record and monitor development.
   - Implementing the development plan.
   - Evaluating the effectiveness of the development plan and the methods used to monitor development.
   - Identifying and justifying decisions relating to future personal development needs.

How are the units assessed?

As you follow the course, you will generate evidence that will be marked by your teacher. This evidence will show that you have achieved all the assessment standards.

Course assessment

The course assessment examines what you have learned in the performance and factors impacting on performance (FIP) units.

This will be assessed through:

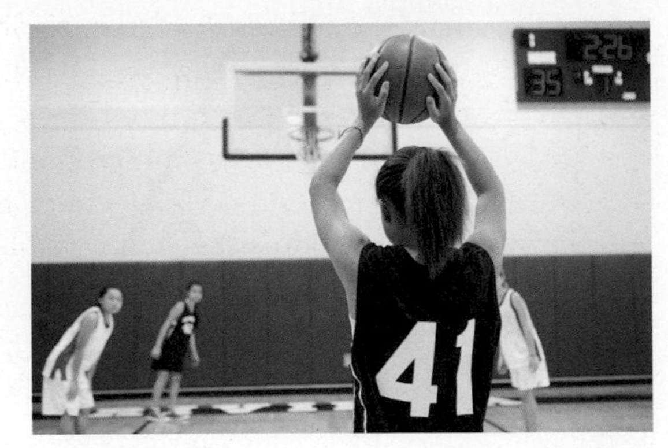

- A single performance event
- An exam.

In the performance element of your PE course, you will be required to take part in a special, one-off performance. This has to be more challenging than the kinds of experiences you will have completed within your performance skills unit.

Your single performance assessment should allow you to demonstrate your best activity.

You will have to consider the three key areas into which this performance will be broken down:

- Planning and preparing for performance – this will involve thinking about what you need to do **before** taking part in your performance assessment. For example, you may have to think about the strengths and weaknesses of your opponent, the music you may use during your dance, or even what type of warm-up is most appropriate for the performance. **This section is worth 8 marks**.
- Carrying out the performance – you will need to show a comprehensive range of movement and performance skills and be able to demonstrate effective decision-making when applying these skills to your performance. **This section is worth 40 marks**.
- Evaluating your performance – this will involve looking back at your performance and thinking about what went well and what did not go so well. **This section is worth 12 marks**.

For the factors impacting on performance (FIP) course assessment you will be required to sit an exam which lasts 1 hour and 30 minutes. This will be completed in school and then marked by SQA. The question paper will examine how well you can do the following:

- Demonstrate a range of approaches for developing or refining skills, fitness and performance composition/tactics.
- Analyse factors that impact on performance.
- Analyse and evaluate factors impacting on your performance to develop personal performance.

The exam will look at the types of things you did to try to improve any of the factors you identified as impacting performance. This is very similar to the assessments you will complete in class to pass the FIP unit. However, although the process in the exam is the same, you will be asked more detailed and different questions requiring you to show how you can apply your knowledge about performance development.

The course assessment you carry out requires you to reflect on the work you did to gather information within the performance development process. As you work to improve your performance, the data you collected, the approaches you used to improve specific factors which impact performance, the way these are used to monitor the progress made while training, and the success achieved as a result of training are all areas that will be examined.

In the 'scenario' part of the exam you will be asked to look at different performance problems and to use the knowledge and skills you have developed to explain potential problems, to suggest solutions and to demonstrate an understanding of how the factors might influence performance. You will be able to use knowledge from different activities and from your use of different approaches to help you investigate and explain reasons why a performance turned out the way it did.

How to use this book

Your teacher will direct you to the chapters that are relevant to your particular course.

Try to read through the information and make use of the activities suggested to help you develop your skills, knowledge and understanding of performance development.

Some of the activities can be completed in a group and you will be able to complete others by yourself.

Use the symbols to guide you through the sections. These are common to all of the factors that impact performance (FIP).

The aim is to help you develop your performance by using the knowledge and skills developed in the FIP unit.

Features of this book

In this chapter you will learn

A list of topics covered in the chapter.

What should I already know?

Throughout this book you will see the symbol above when you are required to reflect back on learning you have completed in earlier years and in other subjects you have studied. This will help you build on skills and knowledge you have gained from your broad general education (BGE) and your National 4 or 5 PE course.

GO! Activity

Tasks that reinforce important knowledge or help you apply the knowledge to other activities in the course. You will do these on your own or with groups to solve problems and develop a range of useful skills.

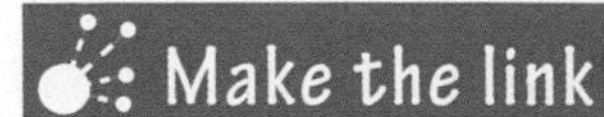

This feature highlights links between the topic you are studying, topics in the book and other subjects you may be studying.

Interesting facts

Facts relating to the knowledge or skills you are focusing on are included – just for fun!

Skills for life, learning and work

Highlights the skills for learning, skills for life and skills for work that you will develop throughout the Higher PE course.

Assessment in PE

When these are included, advice will be given about how you can use the skills and/or knowledge you have developed to achieve the assessment standards which make up the Higher course.

Check your progress

Short questions that test your knowledge of each topic.

HELP NEEDED | *GETTING THERE* | *CONFIDENT*

Thinking skills in PE

All the parts of your course are designed to encourage you to become:

- Successful learners
- Effective contributors
- Responsible citizens
- Confident individuals.

In PE your experiences taking part in activities which form part of your course and in activities you do after or outside school will help you develop physical, emotional, mental and social skills. The processes you go through and the knowledge you gain will help you to complete all the parts of the internal unit assessments and the course assessments.

The range of thinking skills you develop will be common to many of your Higher courses. This will help you to make connections between different subjects and to use skills in both familiar and unfamiliar situations. By doing this you can begin to understand different concepts and move towards being successful in all aspects of your learning.

It is important that you understand that the thinking skills you develop while studying this course will challenge you to think. Sometimes you might only need to **describe** – give details about what something looks like. At other times you will need to **explain** – give details about **why** something is the way it is. You will also be required at Higher to **evaluate** a variety of methods or approaches you have used. This will require you to give benefits and limitations and to assess and make judgements about progress you make while trying to develop your performance. In some areas you will need to demonstrate ability to **analyse**. This will mean you will need to break down information into component parts, or important parts, to inspect or look in detail at methods and approaches you used to develop performance.

Throughout your unit assessments and in preparation for the course assessments you will come across a range of command words which indicate that you should respond in certain ways with the knowledge and skills you have. When you understand what these words mean, you will be able to answer the questions well and achieve high marks. This will be explained more fully in the Rationale for Higher Physical Education chapter.

Skills for learning, skills for life and skills for work

Within the Higher PE course you will develop skills for learning, skills for life and skills for work.

Skills	Focus in PE
Emotional wellbeing	The activities you cover in the course should help you identify your own emotions and feelings and those of others. You will also develop skills to deal with emotions and manage them effectively. In a practical sense, by being able to do this you can start to solve problems and build up a collection of skills that will help you make decisions while performing and help you adapt when things change in a performance situation. These skills help you develop as an all-round performer.
Physical wellbeing	Your physical wellbeing is a primary focus in PE in the Higher course. You will take on responsibility to improve the condition of your body, your overall health and to increase awareness of what steps you can take to get and stay healthy in all of the four factors that impact performance.
Working with others	This is another key area in the Higher course. You will get opportunities to work on your own and with others. In these environments you will develop many different interpersonal skills. These will stand you in good stead when entering the world of work.
Analysing and evaluating	By examining performance development progress you will get the chance to develop skills that help you identify strengths and areas that need development. This will require you to reflect, evaluate and make judgments about the process you went through. These skills can be applied to any area of your life and will ensure that you make judgments based on evidence you gather.

The four factors covered in this book

	The mental factor	The emotional factor	The social factor	The physical factor		
				Fitness	Skills	Tactics/ composition
Feature	Mental state	Self control	Gender issues	Anaerobic endurance	Consistency	Role-related demands
Methods of data collection	POMs	Disciplinary record	Personal reflection	Time related observation schedule	GOS	Game analysis
				PaceTracker App	Skills tests	Team/group feedback
Approaches to develop factors	Aversion training	Positive outlook	Conditioned games	Interval training	Blocked training	Integrated approach
	Reframing	Parking			Variable training	Analytical approach
	Success imagery			Sprinting drills	Random approach	
Feature	Anticipation	Anxiety	Working in isolation	Power	Creativity	Team/group strengths and weaknesses
Methods of data collection	Self reflection	SCAT	Coach feedback	Sargent Jump	Self-assessment	Team/group feedback
Approaches to develop factors	Structured approach	Centering	Referencing approach	Plyometrics	Gradual build-up	Matching approach
	Unstructured approach	PMR	Buddy approach	Ballistics	Improvisation approach	Playing to strengths and avoiding opponents' weaknesses
					Scenario approach	
Feature			Communication	Aerobic endurance		Communication
Methods of data collection			Communication questionnaire	Time-related observation schedule		Communication questionnaire
Approaches to develop factors			Team communication drills	Interval training		Team communication drills
			Conditioned games			Conditioned games

2 Rationale for Higher Physical Education

Mandatory skills, knowledge and understanding

As you work your way through the Higher course, you will learn knowledge and skills that will enable you to develop performance. These are the **mandatory skills, knowledge and understanding** (MSKU).

These MSKU include:

Component 1: performance

Planning and preparation

- Identifying factors impacting on performance: mental, emotional, social and physical factors — the physical factor includes fitness, skills, tactics/composition.
- Understanding the potential impact on performance for each of the following four factors: mental, emotional, social and physical – the impact of these factors could be positive or negative.
- Explaining challenges faced by a performer.
- Planning and preparation for a performance.
- Implementing a performance development plan.

Performance

Learners must demonstrate:

- A repertoire of complex movement and performance skills (physical activity specific).
- Control and fluency of complex movement and performance skills.
- Decision-making and problem solving.
- Rules, regulations and etiquette for physical activities.
- Controlling emotions.
- Working with others.

Evaluation of performance

- Reviewing performance.
- Evaluating performance in terms of strengths and areas for development.
- Identifying future development needs for each of the following factors impacting on performance: mental, emotional, social and physical.

Component 2: question paper

Methods of collecting information to analyse factors impacting on performance

- Reliability, validity, practicability.
- Application of recognised tests or analytical tools for collecting information.
- Appropriateness of methods for collecting information
  – organisational issues of collection methods.
- Use of model performances.
- Interpretation of qualitative, quantitative, objective and subjective information
  – receiving/accepting/giving/timing of feedback.
- Identification of strengths and areas for development.

Approaches to performance development

- Purpose of performance development planning.
- Prioritising of development needs for four factors impacting on performance: mental, emotional, social and physical.
- Potential impacts of mental, emotional, social and physical factors on performance development.
- Performance development goals.
- Approaches to meet performance development goals
  – specificity in the process performance development.

Recording, monitoring and evaluating performance development

- Purpose and value of recording, monitoring and evaluating performance development.
- Key planning information.
- Recording methods or tools.
- Production of performance development plans.
- Implementation of performance development plans.
- Monitoring methods, tests or tools.
- Adapting performance development plans.
- Future performance development planning.

The course will enable you to deepen your learning by encouraging you to apply your knowledge and skills:

- in different activities
- in more than one performance
- alongside knowledge from other experiences
- in a range of situations where decision-making is required
- in a range of situations where you need to solve performance-related problems
- in a range of situations which require you to take on specialised roles.

Course assessment for FIP

In the exam, you will be required to show higher order thinking over and above just 'remembering'. You will be asked to:

- Explain how you gathered information, what made these methods reliable, how the results were accurate
- Justify your choice of approaches to develop your performance within the four MESP factors
- Explain and evaluate the methods you used to monitor and check progress while you were using, and after you finished using, the approaches you chose.

These all require you to develop: **analytical thinking skills and evaluative thinking skills**.

Within the approaches section of the course, you will **investigate** the variety of methods available to assist performance development of the four MESP factors. This will require you to write about:

- why one approach might be more useful than another
- the decisions you made about the changes and adaptations you need to make as you use these approaches
- the similarities and differences between approaches used to develop performance.

Finally, throughout the performance development process you will **critically examine, analyse and evaluate** the progress you make. You will write about:

- the reasons why the approaches made a positive impact on your performance
- the conclusions that can be drawn about the success or otherwise of the approaches you used.

Your teacher will organise lessons that enable you to:

- investigate
- solve problems
- make decisions
- compare methods and approaches
- interpret data
- judge decisions made
- diagnose problems
- break down methods and approaches and find out their parts
- rank methods and approaches.

Course assessment for performance

You will take part in a single event performance similar to the National 5 performance course assessment. You will be assessed in:

- The preparation you undertake to deal with the demands of this special performance. Specifically you will need to show you have:
  1. considered the challenges you anticipate you will face

2. decided on the strategies you intend to put in place to deal with or overcome the challenges you have identified
3. organised and carried out an appropriate warm-up.

- The actual performance – specifically:
  1. the application and use of the correct skills at the correct time consistently throughout the performance
  2. the control and fluency you demonstrate as you perform
  3. the appropriateness of the decisions you **attempt** to carry out as you perform
  4. the **success** of the decisions you take as you perform
  5. your ability to follow the rules and to control your emotions as the performance happens.
- You will also be required to evaluate the performance you gave – specifically:
  1. how you coped with the challenges you anticipated before you began your performance
  2. why the overall performance was successful or not.

To prepare you for this special, single performance event you may have the opportunity to experience scenarios or different types of challenges within other activities which might require you to deal with unforeseen problems. These might include:

- the chance to be exposed to how a performance is affected by the presence of an audience or supporters
- how a performance is affected by an 'unknown' opponent
- how a performance is affected by last-minute changes
- how a performance is affected when the result or outcome is important or perhaps irrelevant
- how a performance is affected when competing against a much stronger or more experienced performer.

The more creative these scenarios are, the more likely it is that you will become skilled in dealing with the demands of different performance environments.

By preparing for and dealing with the range of different performance contexts that you may have to face, you will begin to build an armoury or stockpile of knowledge and skills that can be applied to help you overcome a range of different performance problems.

We can liken it to learning to drive for the first time. The lessons you go through teach you the skills required to take control of the car. Once you have mastered the pedals and steering in a car park, the instructor might let you apply the skills on the drive home. However, to actually pass your driving test, you must develop skills in 'hazard perception'. This means that, as you drive, you must be aware of pedestrians and other traffic – or potential hazards. As you become accustomed to driving, you are able to forget about what your feet and hands must do and focus on the conditions you are driving in, the traffic lights up ahead, etc. You must think ahead and try to consider what other hazards, such as pedestrians and other traffic, might do. Therefore, you are prepared if and when you have to make a split-second decision.

Transfer this back into a performance situation. As you learn to 'read' what you anticipate is going to happen, or deal with what actually does happen, you become more skilled in solving performance problems because you have faced them or something similar before.

A very skilled performer can use prior learning to deal with even the most unusual or unexpected occurrence.

The preparation and lessons you experience as you prepare for the single performance event should equip you with problem-solving skills that you can then call upon to help you face challenges.

This will be useful for you when you sit your Higher course exam. In the 'scenario' part of the paper, you will need to use your knowledge and skills to solve a performance problem.

You will reflect back on which factors impacted your single performance event, what decisions you had to take to help you overcome the impact of these factors and give accurate evaluations about how successful these decisions were.

Therefore, when the scenario questions ask you to anticipate what action you **might** take, and which factors **might** be influencing a given performance, you will already have had exposure to a useful 'bank' of performance problems and their associated possible solutions.

By applying this knowledge and using the thinking skills you have developed, you will be successful in the exam.

speedo

Factors impacting on performance

3 Factors impacting on performance

In this chapter you will learn:

1. The impact of different factors on live performance.
2. To identify the types of performance problems which might impact a 'live' performance.

Fundamentals of the factors

In order to make sense of the four main factors it would be wise to understand the key focus for each area.

The **mental** factor concerns all cognitive processing involved with performance.

Therefore a checklist of knowledge you will cover for the mental factor is likely to be:

- How to collect information relating to this factor.
- The impact on performance of mental features being under control and at optimum levels.
- The approaches which can be used to develop mental features.
- How to monitor performance development.
- Justification of future needs following performance development.

The **emotional** factor concerns the main emotions and their impact on performance.

Therefore a checklist of knowledge you will cover for the mental factor is likely to be:

- How to collect information relating to happiness, anger, fear, trust or surprise.
- The impact on performance of emotional features being under control and at optimum levels.
- The approaches which can be used to develop emotional features.
- How to monitor performance development.
- Justification of future needs following performance development.

The **social** factor concerns the impact others and societal/ environmental issues can have on our performance.

Therefore a checklist of knowledge you will cover for the social factor is likely to be:

- How to collect information relating to this factor.
- The impact on performance of others, societal/ environmental issues.
- The approaches that can be used to develop social features.
- How to monitor performance development.
- Justification of future needs following performance development.

The **physical** factor concerns everything to do with physical fitness, skill development and tactics or compositional elements of performance.

When studying this area you will probably only look at around two or three features in total.

Therefore a checklist of knowledge you will cover for the physical factor is likely to be:

- Physical and skill-related aspects of fitness.
- The impact on performance of aspects of fitness.
- How to collect information relating to these aspects of fitness.
- Principles of training.
- Approaches to develop aspects of fitness.
- How to monitor performance development.
- Justification of future needs following performance development.

OR

- Types of skills.
- The impact on performance of different types of skill and their effectiveness.
- How to collect information about these skills.
- Stages of learning.
- Qualities of effective performance.
- Approaches to develop skills.
- How to monitor performance development.
- Justification of future needs following performance development.

OR

- Effective strategies, formations and/or compositions incorporating the principles of play.
- The impact on performance of different strategies, tactics, formations and/or comparisons.

- How to collect information relating to these strategies, tactics, formations and/or compositions.
- Performance considerations.
- Approaches to deal with performance considerations.
- Choreographic devices.
- How to monitor performance development.
- Justification of future needs following performance development.

Factors – course assessment

Your lessons will be structured to enable you to experience a real live performance situation and all the challenges you will need to face.

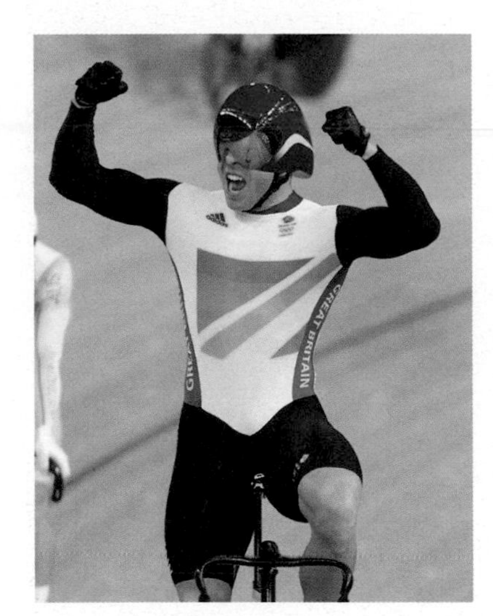

You will prepare for the single event performance much like an athlete preparing for the Commonwealth or Olympic Games, a League qualifying game, a District Cup competition or important gala.

You will prepare **mentally**, **emotionally**, **socially** and **physically**.

Your lessons will expose you to a range of situations, occurrences and experiences that you might never have faced before. In this way, you will become aware of areas in your performance that need attention, areas which could affect you winning or losing and areas that you can use to maximise your chances of success. Having taken part in these lessons you will then be able to identify parts of your performance you need to address **before** you are assessed in your one-off course assessment.

This will help you achieve more marks from the 60 that are available. The work you do in your FIP should help prepare you to take action to improve some of the areas that have been identified as requiring attention. By planning and putting in place approaches to improve your identified development needs, you will have an overall positive impact on this one-off assessment.

Therefore the specific areas you identify really need you to set goals that are **SMART**:

- **S**pecific to you.
- **M**easurable so that we can see the improvements you make as you implement the approaches you have decided to use.
- **A**ttainable goals that are **R**ealistic to you in the role you have to carry out within your performance and achievable within the time you have in your course.
- **T**imed and targeted over a period of time so that you have something (a goal) to focus and work towards.

The overall intention is to get as high a mark as possible in your one-off performance assessment. The course is designed to let all students work towards a special performance regardless of the level at which they play or the competitions in which they take part. By personalising the activity you choose to use and the needs you have chosen to work on, every performer can set about improving their own performance.

You will use your time in class:

- Improving your performance by working towards personal development targets
- Getting experience dealing with performance problems.

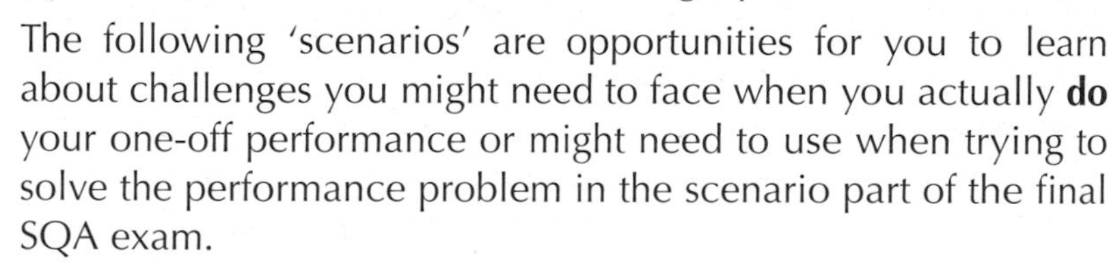

Performance is at the heart of the Higher course. You will therefore need to gain a pass in two activities to achieve a unit pass for performance as well as participating in a special, challenging performance in your best activity. Everything you learn in the FIP and Performance units will be focusing on giving you the knowledge you need to help you make use of the skills you are developing. This will enable you to gain the greatest success in your course assessments (exam and single performance event).

The following 'scenarios' are opportunities for you to learn about challenges you might need to face when you actually **do** your one-off performance or might need to use when trying to solve the performance problem in the scenario part of the final SQA exam.

Each of the scenarios will expose you to a range of **factors** that might influence the outcome of your performance. There are suggested approaches which might be included in an integrated training programme or used on their own as stand-alone approaches so that your overall performance has the best chance possible of improving.

A performer would never focus solely on just one area of their performance. Overall they need to look at everything that can be finely tuned to ensure they are in tip top condition mentally, emotionally, socially and physically – no area is neglected.

It could be that there are four different approaches being used to deal with each of the factors – there could be even more. Variety is incredibly important when you begin to plan and prepare to improve your performance; this is how motivation and focus is maintained throughout a long season.

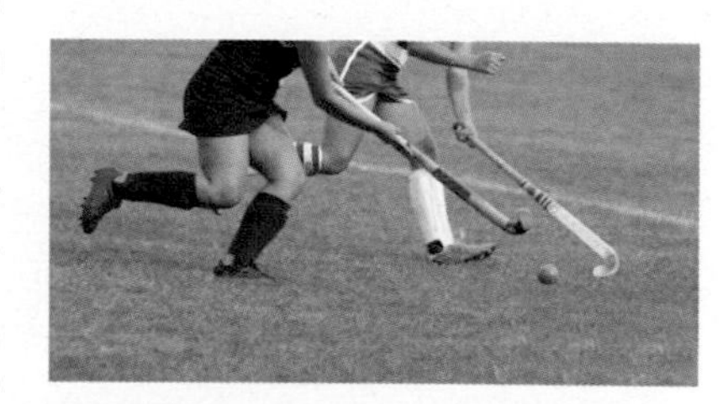

The suggested scenarios give a little detail about how all four factors can have an impact within different challenges. By considering how these factors influence performance you will begin to acquire knowledge about what the different challenges are, what problems might have to be faced and what approaches might help develop the skills to deal with these problems.

Hopefully, by working through some of these challenges you will develop a better understanding of what performance problems you might need to think about, to adapt to and to deal with in your own activities.

Your teacher may use all, some or none of these scenarios.

Activities	Challenge
Dance/creative activities	Dealing with a 'planned' audience
	Dealing with an 'unplanned' audience
	Position of 'front' changed at last minute
	One of the performers being in the wrong place or doing the wrong step during the performance
	A member of the group/team being injured during the performance
Games	Crowd present
	Very early goal won or lost
	Injury to key player
	Significant substitution by opposition
	One player in your team having a 'nightmare'
	Fouls picked up very early on in match
	Change of strategy by opposition
	Opposition target one of your players
	Weather conditions change
	Last minute changes to tactics
	Time running out during match

Look at the pages of the scenarios that suit the activities you are covering in your course. You will see that the performance problems these scenarios give you can be attributed to one or more of the factors that impact on the success of your performance. That is, it could be:

- A **mental** issue
- An **emotional** issue
- A **social** issue
- A skill issue
- A tactical or compositional issue
- A fitness issue.

(The last three: } A **physical** issue)

Here are some general performance problems:

			Physical Factor		
Mental	**Emotional**	**Social**	**Skill**	**Tactical/Compositional**	**Fitness**
Situation too stressful	Lack of self-belief	Fall out among friends	Injury	Box + 1	Can't keep up
Don't care	Go 'down' after losing first few points	Influential player missing	Forced to play weak stroke	Full court man to man	Too strong opposition
Couple of bad decisions	Get angry and frustrated	Someone doesn't care enough	Play against a left hander	Double block	Too fast opposition
Lose focus	Panic in the first five minutes			Use of rugby chairlift for netball	
Crack under pressure	Lack of trust between players				
Don't see what the opposition are doing	Don't deal with the element of surprise well				

There are many more examples of how performance is affected by the four factors. These would affect the decisions you would need to consider making **before** you begin the performance. Plans could be changed about, for example, who plays where, who marks who, what stroke should be exploited, what passes should be avoided, how many strokes are to be taken under water.

Decisions made before a performance can be as a result of something that affects only you, something you might anticipate the opposition doing, or even something that affects all performers.

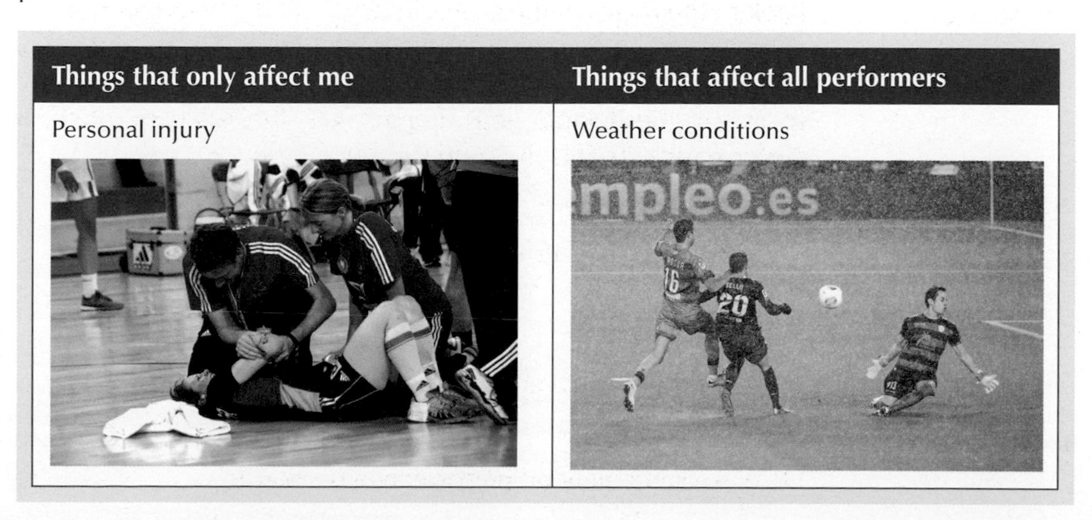

Things that only affect me	Things that affect all performers
Personal injury	Weather conditions

Activity 3.1

In your activities, list the kinds of performance issues that can affect **just you** and the kinds of things that have an effect on **you and the other performers**.

Considering the impact of different factors on your own and on others' performance means you are able to plan, make changes or adaptations so that the performance you give is the best possible. This will help you plan effectively for your single performance event 'Planning Stage' where there are 8 marks available and also analyse and answer the scenario performance problem part of your final exam.

Performance context 1: dealing with a planned audience

Mental issues that might affect performance –

- The presence of an audience might affect your concentration and levels of arousal and your ability to make the correct decisions while performing.

How would this impact on actual performance?

- There might be people/friends in the audience, which could intimidate you. These people might encourage you or they might make you feel fearful of making mistakes (mental toughness).
- You might make rushed passes or lose your opponent or not move at the right time to complete a part of a motif with a partner, or double up to block an incoming spike (anticipation).

What approaches could you use to help you overcome these issues?

- Rehearsed performances with a range of audiences.
- Simulated drills to assist with pressured features within a game.

Emotional issues that might affect performance –

- Before, during or even after the performance your emotions could become out of control, due to nerves or anxiety.

How would this impact on actual performance?

- Before going on to compete, you might not be able to listen to the instructions about where to play, or how to correct a part of a sequence that was done badly last performance (self-control).
- You might react badly to being left off the starting line up (aggression).
- You might feel tearful or incapable of giving your best (anxiety).

What approaches could you use to help you overcome these issues?

- Deep breathing.
- Visualisation.

Social issues that might affect performance –

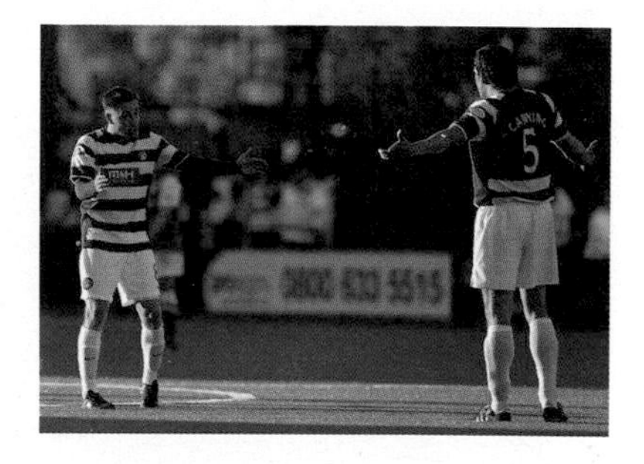

- The audience/crowd might add to the stress levels and mean you might have had a disagreement with one of your group before the performance began (peer groups, group dynamics, gender issues).

How would this impact on actual performance?

- The group dynamic would change. There might be animosity between team/group members, which might mean people are reluctant to pass the ball to another team member, people might get frustrated easily at each other and further negative consequences could occur.

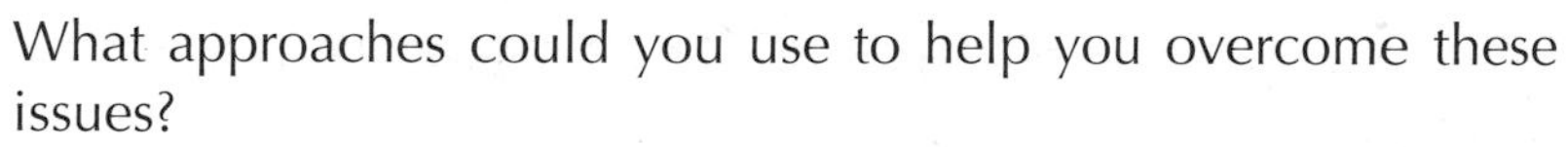

What approaches could you use to help you overcome these issues?

- Parking.
- Positive team talk.
- Conditioned games.

Physical (fitness) issues that might affect performance –

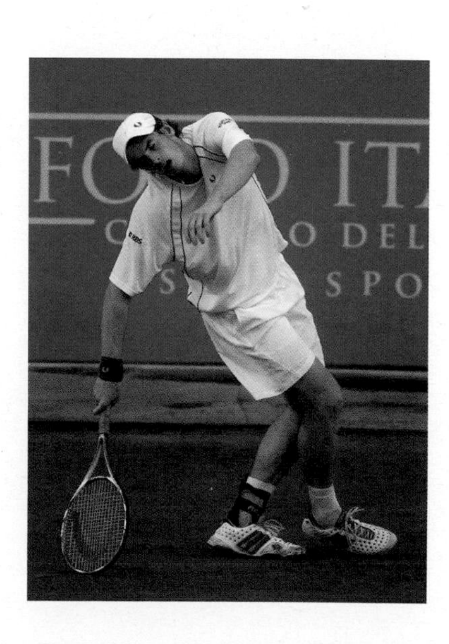

- The audience may witness you being unable to make enough powerful sprints or keep the tempo high throughout the whole performance (anaerobic endurance).
- When required you may not be able to jump high enough throughout the performance or hit/throw the ball quickly and powerfully enough (power).

How would this impact on actual performance?

- Opponents would be able to get away from you, timing might be affected if jumps are not high enough.
- Blocking, rebounding and keeping possession of the ball might be an issue while performing.

What approaches could you use to help you overcome these issues?

- Interval training.
- Plyometrics.

Physical (skill) issues that might affect performance –

- The quality of passes/strokes is inconsistent throughout the performance (consistency) due to the stress associated with the presence of the audience.
- Joining skills together when required is problematic (fluency) again, due to nerves.

How would this impact on actual performance?

- Points, goals, possession would be surrendered giving the opposition the chance to counter attack.
- Points would be lost in aesthetic activities; moving with a ball or moving to hit a moving object would likely be unsuccessful.

What approaches could you use to help you overcome these issues?

- Progressive programme of skills drills.
- Gradual build-up.

Physical (tactical/compositional) issues that might affect performance –

- There might be confusion about different responsibilities within a team/group (role related demands) because of the audience being present.
- Improvisation might not be encouraged within the performance.

How would this impact on actual performance?

- People could be in the wrong place at the wrong time; this could mean people are left unmarked or the wrong decision is taken about where to stand on receipt of service.
- In team competitive games this might disadvantage and dishearten creative players.
- In creative activities motivation levels might be low because the performer had no input into the sequences/ choreographies.

What approaches could you use to help you overcome these issues?

- Variable training or scenario approach to help groups work through the range of situations which might occur.

Performance context 2: dealing with an unplanned audience

Mental issues that might affect performance –

- The late arrival of an audience or spectators while a performance is taking place might affect concentration and distract you from what you should be focusing on.

How would this impact on actual performance?

- Your decision-making might be flawed as you miss where a player is running to or where the ball is being played. This could mean a player is left unmarked momentarily and might have an easy shot on goal. A dancer who for an instant loses concentration and focus could mistime a move or turn in the wrong direction. This would make the dance look messy and perhaps mean others in the group need to adjust what they are doing to cope with the mistake you make.

What approaches could you use to help you overcome these types of issues?

- Rehearsed performances in class time with people coming and going during the actual performance.

Emotional issues that might affect performance –

- Panic might occur as you realise you have lost concentration having been momentarily distracted by the arrival of an audience/spectator.

How would this impact on actual performance?

- You might lose the person you were marking, might give away possession of the ball or miss the opportunity to play a shot into a vacant space on court.

What approaches could you use to help you overcome these types of issues?

- Use pressure drills where performers need to focus on given directions or make lots of decisions quickly when under pressure.

Social issues that might affect performance –

- As players or performers make mistakes, they contribute less to the overall performance and are in fact less in control of their own actions.

How would this impact on actual performance?

- Points might be lost, players might lose faith in each other and stop giving passes to the player they feel is letting the team down. This player might then become a weak link and feel excluded from the team.
- In creative group activities a weak link might mean the group does not function as a unit and might then not encourage others to do their best.

What approaches could you use to help you overcome these issues?

- Conditioned games might be used to allow performers to 'rehearse' in training the variety of things which could go wrong with team errors.

Physical (fitness) issues that might affect performance –

- Reaction time and anticipation might be affected.

How would this impact on actual performance?

- Being distracted might mean the performer is slow to react to the spike coming over the net or a gap in the wall being set by a defence. This would mean the opposition could exploit a space or player who was not focused on the performance.

What approaches could you use to help you overcome these issues?

- Use improvisation approach where players are expected to cope with elements of play that the opposition might disguise.

Physical (skill) issues that might affect performance –

- Consistency might be affected if a player or performer is distracted during performance.

How would this impact on actual performance?

- A player whose shooting becomes erratic and inconsistent during play might be substituted.

What approaches could you use to help you overcome these types of issues?

- Use pressure drills to prepare for dealing with this type of situation and to increase consistency.

Physical (tactical/compositional) issues that might affect performance –

- Rhythm and flair might be affected when a performer is distracted by an unplanned interruption of this sort.

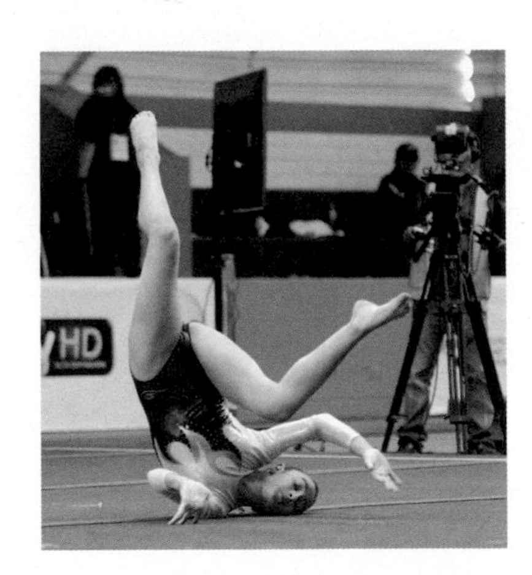

How would this impact on actual performance?

- The planned execution of stroke patterns would be interrupted and so consistency and control of rally might be affected. In dance or gymnastics routine the flow of the skills would be more disjointed and less smooth.

What approaches could you use to help you overcome these issues?

- Use scenario or variable training that includes interruptions when training to prepare for thought process or concentration being affected.

Performance context 3: Position of front is changed

Mental issues that might affect performance –

- Perception of where a dancer was as she turned and tried to get her bearings to begin her next movement.

How would this impact on actual performance?

- Confusion might occur and the overall performance would look messy and probably less precise.

What approaches could you use to help you overcome these types of issues?

- Practise the dance using different 'fronts'.

Emotional issues that might affect performance –

- The dancer might become anxious about beginning her performance and as the dance progressed this anxiety might build, resulting in confusion and indecision.

How would this impact on actual performance?

- Dancers might move in the wrong direction or be unsure which motif is to be performed to which 'front'.

What approaches could you use to help you overcome these types of issues?

- Practise the dance using a variety of 'fronts'.

Social issues that might affect performance –

- When an element such as the 'front' is changed the group dynamic might alter and some dancers might become uncertain and indecisive about where they should be facing during different parts of the dance.

How would this impact on actual performance?

- The overall appearance of the dance might be affected as indecision can make the dancers hesitate about where to face. The dance might then be out of time or movements, which are intended to be performed together, are out of synchronisation. This would make the dance look less appealing and less interesting.

What approaches could you use to help you overcome these types of issues?

- Coached classes where the teacher might forewarn the group that a turn to the right was next.
- Rehearsing the dance using different fronts would help.

Physical (fitness) issues that might affect performance –

- Balance and coordination might be affected.

How would this impact on actual performance?

- Holding a balance or moving into or out of the balance could be less successful and consequently affect the timing of the next part of the sequence.

What approaches could you use to help you overcome these types of issues?

- Work through a series of balances using different fronts, changing the directions of the 'front'.

Physical (skill) issues that might affect performance –

- The quality of the performance might be affected and so it might deteriorate technically.

How would this impact on actual performance?

- The timing of jumps, turns and motifs would be affected and so the dance might not fit together smoothly or be in time to the music.

What approaches could you use to help you overcome these types of issues?

- Rehearse the dance using different fronts, getting feedback as you perform to ensure you stay in time with the music.

Physical (tactical/compositional) issues that might affect performance –

- When repetition is being used it is possible that a performer, who miscounts the number of repetitions due to being distracted, could interrupt the overall positive flow of a dance.

How would this impact on actual performance?

- This would reduce the impact of the repetitive motif and could make the dance look disorganised and untidy.

What approaches could you use to help you overcome these types of issues?

- Rehearse the dance using different fronts with input from an observer who could count out the number of repetitions to make sure the correct number were being repeated.

Performance context 4: One of the performers being in the wrong place or doing the wrong step during the performance

Mental issues that might affect performance –

- A dancer might miss her cue while dancing with a partner.

How would this impact on actual performance?

- There might be confusion about how to restart the dance or to try to cover for the mistake. This would make the dance look less fluent and less interesting.

What approaches could you use to help you overcome these issues?

- Rehearse the dance regularly with planned action – when mistakes are made, the dancer who has made the mistake picks up immediately on what her partner is doing with the minimum of fuss, and sees the dance through to completion.

Emotional issues that might affect performance –

- The performer's resilience might be affected after an obvious error.

How would this impact on actual performance?

- The performer might walk off stage and leave the performance unfinished.

What approaches could you use to help you overcome these issues?

- Rehearse consistently and when mistakes are made be determined to complete the whole performance.

Social issues that might affect performance –

- When working in a group, there is a social responsibility towards all group members. A performer who does not take this responsibility seriously when they make a mistake will let others down.

How would this impact on actual performance?

- When a mistake is made the 'offending' performer might walk off leaving the remainder of the group in disarray. This would add to the confusion and might even mean the remaining performers could not finish the performance.

What approaches could you use to help you overcome these issues?

- Agree and rehearse a 'park it' strategy before performing so that if someone makes a mistake everyone will try to carry on as best as possible, minimising the disruption to the performance.

Physical (fitness) issue that might affect performance –

- The performer might not have the required endurance levels to keep up with play or sustain the whole performance.

How would this impact on actual performance?

- The player would leave their opponent unmarked allowing them to penetrate.
- A dancer or gymnast would tire near the end of the sequence or performance with movements not being completed to the same high standards as at the beginning of the performance.

What approaches could you use to help you overcome these issues?

- A programme of interval training could be completed to improve speed endurance.

Physical (skill) issues that might affect performance –

- The performer might not have the actual technical capabilities required to enable them to get into the correct position, or the skill that is required to be used in that situation might be too difficult for them.

How would this impact actual performance?

- The type of set given to a player as he approaches for a spike might require him to slow down his preparatory jump in order to connect with the ball at the correct height.
- The dancer might not understand that for a particular position she must hold the contraction in her pelvis in order to make the correct shape.

What approaches could you use to help you overcome these issues?

- A training programme using gradual build-up might be used to introduce a variety of sets during a spiking practice.
- The skill giving a problem would be practised in isolation and then inserted back into the dance.

Physical (tactical/compositional) issues that might affect performance –

- The result of the previous performance was very negative.

How would this impact actual performance?

- The team or group were very generous in estimating the strength of the opposition and so might go out and play a very defensive strategy.
- In creative activities this might mean too easy a sequence or dance would be organised where only low points were possible.

What approaches could you use to help you overcome these issues?

- Observe the performance via video to be sure the strengths are identified accurately and plans put in place to try to minimise the effects of these strengths.
- Plan to include some more complex skills that the performer is confident with in order to get a balance of simple and complex skills to be able to access higher marks.

Here are other performance contexts you might consider in your preparation for your final exam:

Performance context 5 – The opposition take the lead very early on during a match

Performance context 6 – A significant substitution is made by the opposition

Performance context 7 – One player in the team or group is performing very badly

Performance context 8 – The opposition change strategy

Performance context 9 – Opposition targets a particular player or exploits a weakness in the team's play

Performance context 10 – Time is running out in the match and you are winning/losing

Performance context 11 – The sprinter is in the lead in the first 15 metres of the 100 metres

Performance context 12 – Captain is sent off.

The scenario part of the exam requires you to try to use the knowledge and skills you have developed to analyse a performance problem and to try to find possible solutions or explanations as to why a performance is impacted in different ways.

Evaluating the impact of factors on performance

Assessment in PE

1.2 Evaluating the impact of positive and negative factors on a performance

Judging the number of times or trying to qualify how much your performance is affected positively or negatively will allow you to achieve this assessment standard.

The illustration below gives an overview of how mental, emotional, social and physical factors can impact on your performance positively or negatively. During the Higher course, you must consider the impact these factors have on your selected performance.

Mental factor	Positive impact on performance
Anticipation 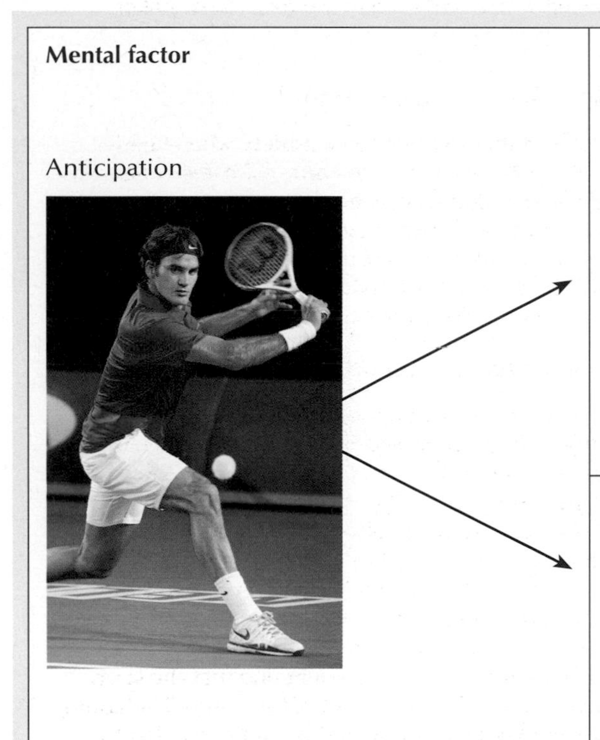	Being able to predict your opponent's next move, or the time in a race when it would be best to make your move, can have a positive impact on your performance. If you can anticipate your opponent's next shot in tennis, through looking at the cues from his body language, racquet position and body position, it will allow you extra time to close down the court and restrict his options. Your ability to anticipate will give you extra time to consider what decisions you need to make next in order to gain an advantage in your performance.
	Negative impact on performance If you are unable to anticipate effectively, you will not be able to plan and prepare for your next response in performance situations. For example, during a game of tennis, if you are unable to anticipate your opponent's next shot, you will be slow to move into the correct ready position, or not have enough time to think about what shot you should play. This will have a negative impact on your performance, as it will result in missed shots and points.

Mental factor	**Positive impact on performance**
Mental toughness	Being determined to succeed, no matter what challenges you face, will have a positive impact on your performance. During your performance development, you will be faced with many challenges and pressures that need to be addressed and converted into responses that could potentially enhance your performance. Being prepared to respond to these challenges positively will allow you to be more in control of your performance. For example, during a long badminton match, which has run into several games and has challenged you both mentally and physically, you will have the mental toughness to stick in and gain a positive result.
	Negative impact on performance If you allow the challenges and pressures you face in your performance development to affect you mentally, it can have a significant impact on the rest of your performance. You may give up early or become completely de-motivated. You might lose focus and concentration and therefore make silly mistakes.

Emotional factor	**Positive impact on performance**
Anxiety 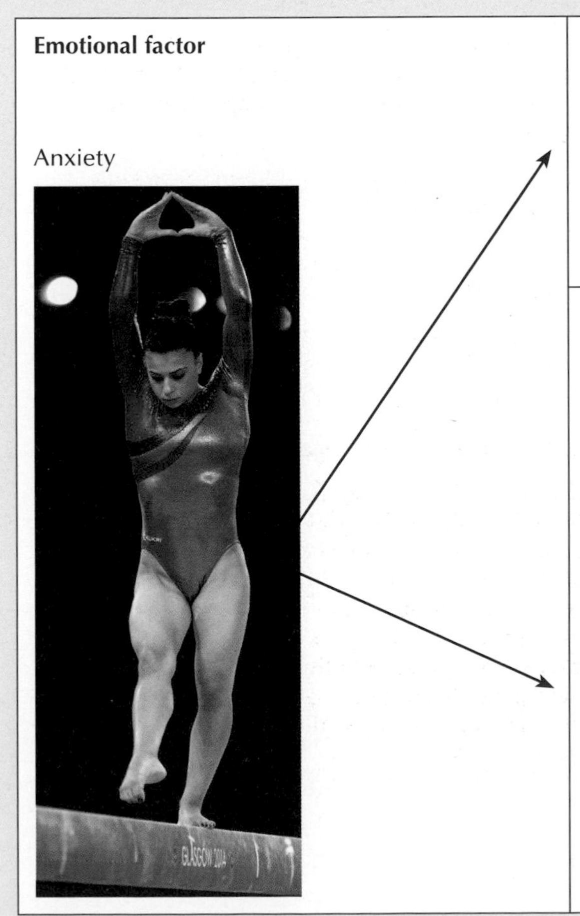	All performers will feel some anxiety when taking part in sport. Being able to control the level of anxiety and channel that anxiety into your performance can have a positive impact on your performance. Some performers feel 'pumped up' before a performance, which if managed correctly can allow you to immediately take control of the performance situation.
	Negative impact on performance When anxiety is not managed correctly, it can have a negative impact on your performance. High levels of anxiety can result in a performer being unable to co-ordinate movements, especially if her body is full of tension. Anxiety can also create negative thoughts, which can impact negatively on performance. They can make a performer doubt her own ability and lead to low self-esteem. In Dance, a performer will have repeated motifs in practice and managed them successfully. However, she might find that she starts to worry about failing in front of the group. This could result in a performance that does not reflect her true capabilities and the work she has put in. When anxiety is not managed correctly, it can have a negative impact on your performance.

(*continued*)

Emotional factor	**Positive impact on performance**
Self-control 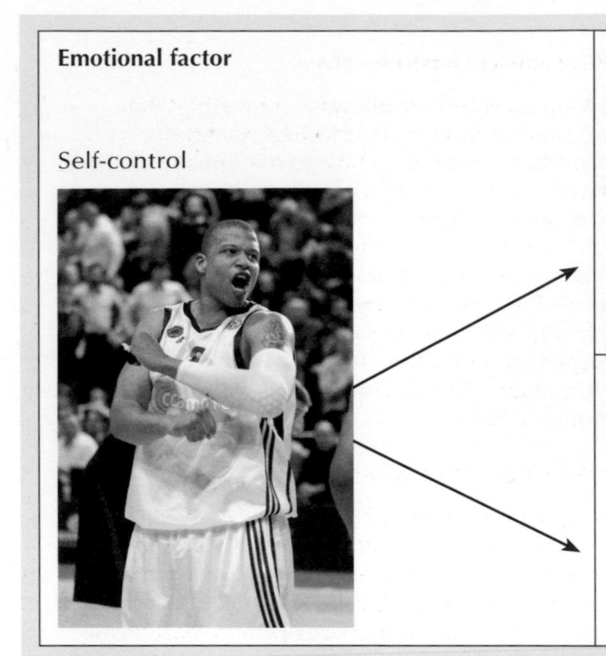	During performance, you may, on occasions, have to show some form of aggression. For example, becoming angry when an opponent steals the ball from you during a basketball game can be effective if you can control that aggression, and channel it into being determined to move back into defence and steal it back. This can have a positive impact on your performance, as it allows you to show self-control and determination during your performance.
	Negative impact on performance
	A performer may be involved in highly pressurised situations where they feel angry. If a performer is unable to control himself, it may lead to disciplinary measures being taken by the referee or official.

Social factor	**Positive impact on performance**
Gender issues 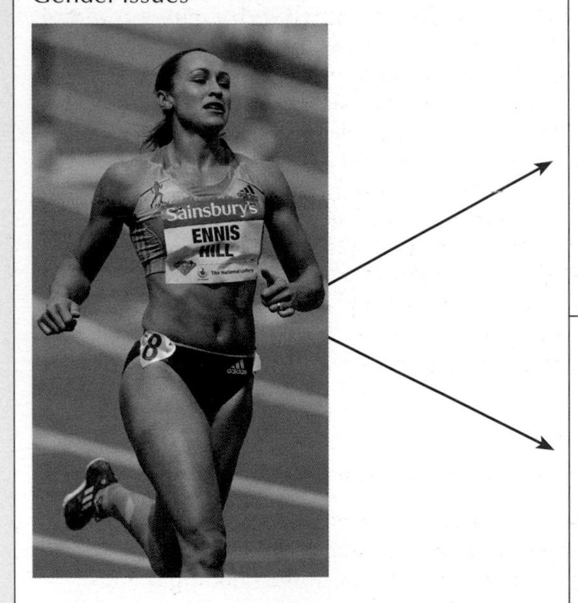	For female athletes, selecting activities that highlight and build on the strengths of female anatomy can have a positive impact on performance. For example, many women have a range of flexibility and balance which allows them to successfully perform a skilled routine on the gymnastics beam. They are able to demonstrate a wide range of complex skills within their performance and show increased control and fluency. This impacts positively on their gymnastic performance as they could gain extra marks. Also, by taking part in sport, women have opportunities to meet role models/female athletes with whom to take their activity forward.
	Negative impact on performance
	Female performance in sport does not always receive the same focus in the media as male sport. There is less coverage of female sport in the media and often lower prize money. Also, occasionally, less value is placed on girls/women achieving high levels of performance compared to males. Over a period of time, these challenges can affect performers' self-esteem and desire to perform successfully or even at all. This lack of self-belief impacts negatively on their performances and might even mean they resist getting involved in any physical activity.

Social factor

Working in isolation

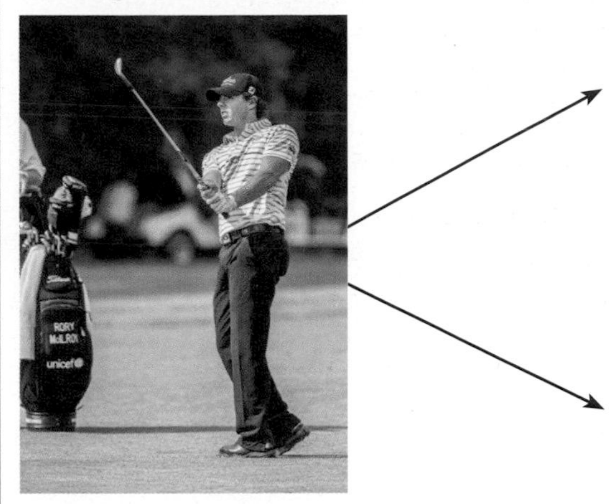

Positive impact on performance

Working on your own allows you to completely focus on your personal performance and the approaches you need to take to continually improve. At times you may wish to concentrate on a specific part of your performance, one that requires your undivided attention to the approaches you have decided to use. For example, some of the mental rehearsal techniques require concentration. If successful, this type of approach will allow you to manage your emotions successfully during your performance – this will impact positively on your performance.

Negative impact on performance

When performing in an individual activity, on many occasions you will be working in isolation during your performance, with no coach or peer feedback. This can have a negative impact on performance, especially if you are trying to improve a part of your performance that has not been successful. You may feel quite isolated as you have little support in your attempts to improve.

Social factor

Communication

This feature can be covered within the social OR physical factor

Positive impact on performance

Your ability to use a variety of verbal and non verbal communication in a positive manner will allow you to feel much more part of the team or contribute more efficiently to the performance. If you are able to communicate your points and be able to listen to others, it will have a positive impact on your performance, as you will be able to interact more effectively and enhance team cohesion and performance. For example, in netball, being able to communicate the next set piece or listen to other teammates when an opponent is not being marked will give you the added opportunity of making sure that all of your team are carrying out their responsibilities correctly.

Negative impact on performance

Being unable to communicate effectively within your performance can impact your ability to feel part of the team and your understanding of the performance. This will in turn impact on your ability to problem solve during your performance, as you will be less effective when trying to discuss key issues with other performers. You will be unable to make clear evaluative comments about your performance, which will impact negatively on your next steps.

Physical factor	Impact on performance
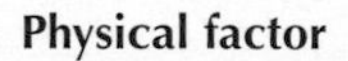 **Physical factor** Anaerobic endurance 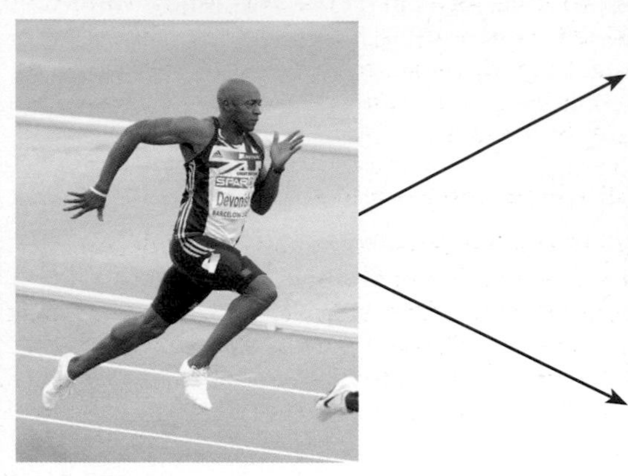	**Positive impact on performance** Being able to work 'without oxygen' during short bursts of intense performance can have a positive impact on your performance. For example, during a sprint in athletics or having to sprint during a performance will require you to have a good level of anaerobic endurance. Anaerobic endurance will allow you to slow down the build-up of lactic acid and improve your ability to sprint throughout a performance, therefore impacting positively on your performance. **Negative impact on performance** Having a decreased level of anaerobic endurance will result in a quicker build-up of lactic acid, which causes muscle fatigue. This can impact your performance negatively, as you will be unable to accelerate or use speed effectively during performances.
Physical factor Power 	**Positive impact on performance** Some performances require you to create strong movements that are performed with speed. For example, if you are able to create strength and speed whilst driving in golf, it will have a positive impact on your performance – you will be able to hit the ball further. Speed and strength allow you to generate a strong action from your core, which will result in you generating club head speed. This will give you greater distance on the golf ball. **Negative impact on performance** If you lack explosive power in your performance, then you will be unable to use strength over a short period of time. This can have a negative impact on your performance, as you will be unable to use fast and powerful movements effectively in your performance. For example, during the high jump you must be able to convert your speed and strength into explosive power when jumping over the bar.
Physical factor Consistency in skill 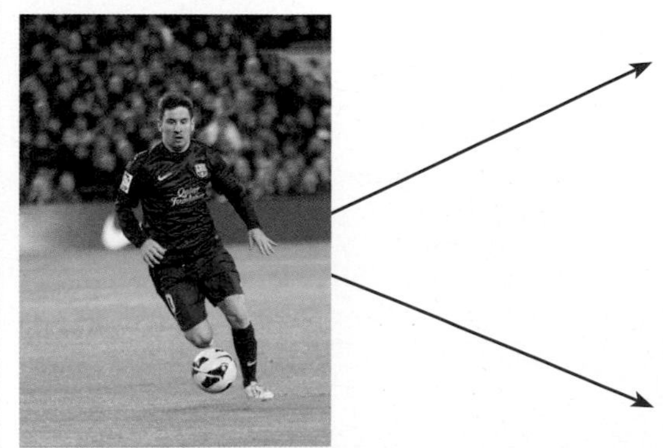	**Positive impact on performance** If you are able to perform consistently in your performances, you can rely and count on the skills you perform. This will have a positive impact on your performance, as you will be able to perfect a range of skills that you require and can be used with success throughout a performance. **Negative impact on performance** When your performance lacks consistency it can have a negative impact on your performance. If you are unable to use your skills consistently you will make more errors and be less dependable and successful.

<table>
<tr>
<td rowspan="2">Physical factor

Creativity
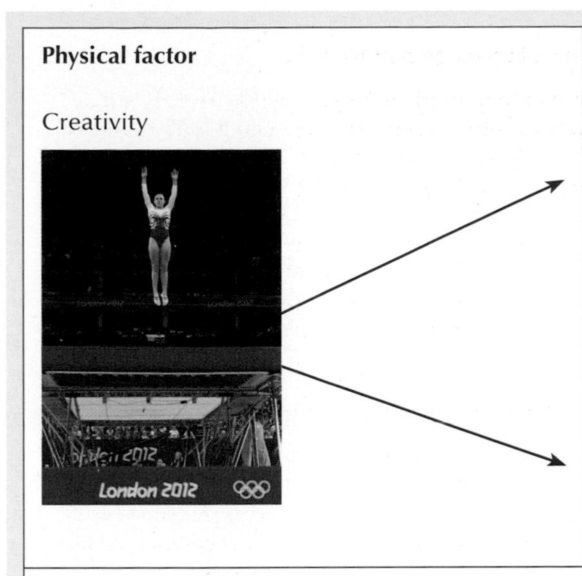
</td>
<td>Positive impact on performance

When being creative in an aesthetic activity, e.g. gymnastics, dance and trampolining, creativity makes your performance look interesting, varied and pleasing to watch. In a game, creativity makes you difficult to mark, makes any opposition uncertain of what you are going to do next and generally makes you unpredictable.</td>
</tr>
<tr>
<td>Negative impact on performance

If your performance lacks creativity overall you will be predictable, repetitive and uninteresting. Opponents would find it easy to anticipate your next move and easily dispossess you or close you down. A dance with little creativity may make the overall performance look boring, causing any audience to switch off.</td>
</tr>
<tr>
<td rowspan="2">Physical factor

Role-related demands
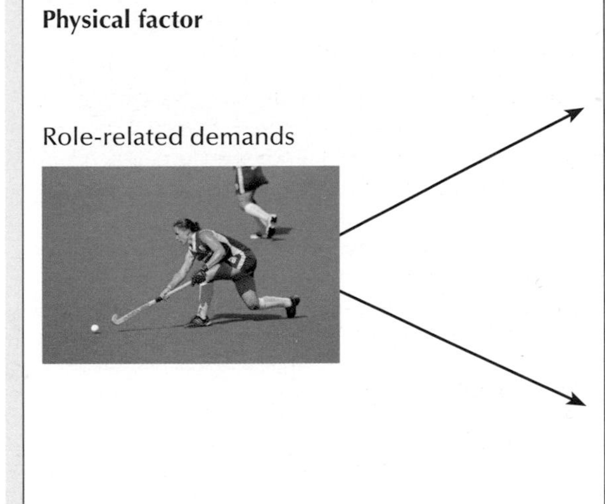</td>
<td>Positive impact on performance

During your performance, you will be faced with specific role-related demands, i.e. certain duties associated with the role you need to carry out. In hockey, at set piece, you may be required to inject the ball out at penalty corners fast and accurately to the top of the circle to the stick stopper. In your role of centre midfield, one of your defensive tasks may be to close down and deny space to the opposition's playmaker.</td>
</tr>
<tr>
<td>Negative impact on performance

If you are unable to grasp the role-related demands of your role, you will become confused and unable to perform effectively with other members in a group/team. This will have a negative impact on your performance, as you will not feel part of your team/ group and your team will be unable to carry out their collective performance effectively, e.g. teammates may not pass to you and you may be substituted.</td>
</tr>
</table>

(*continued*)

Physical Factor	**Positive impact on performance**
Team/group strengths and weaknesses 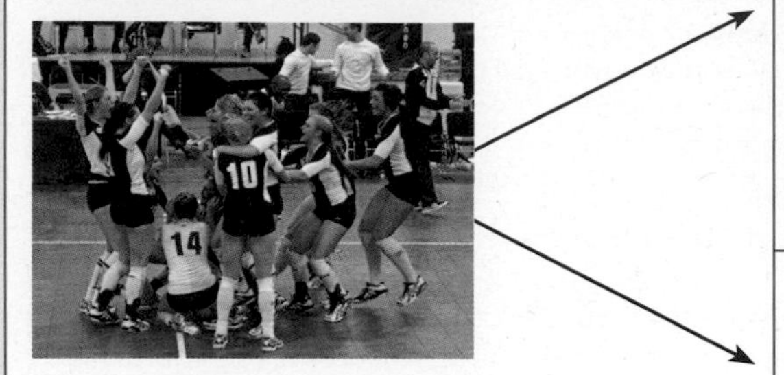	Within a team or group it would be wise to use your strengths to your advantage. This would mean play could be dictated by a strong player or by using a strong stroke. This would make it difficult for the opposition to cope. In an aesthetic activity, e.g. dance, gymnastics and trampolining, specific effective skills could be used within a sequence or motif to make it more interesting or complex. This would make the overall performance look better and achieve higher points or scores.
	Negative impact on performance
	If an opponent could pinpoint your weaknesses it is likely they would try to exploit these. This would almost certainly mean you would be forced to play your weak stroke, the ball might be played to your weakest player, or to an area on the court that was difficult for you to reach. It is also possible that the opposition could limit your ability to use your strengths – making it difficult for you to take control of your own performance. Again this would mean you would lose some control of your performance and possibly your overall game plan or strategy.
Physical factor	**Positive impact on performance**
Communication This feature can be covered within the social OR physical factor 	If communication within a group/team is positive and productive it means any game plan or composition is likely to be successful. Communication before, during and after the performance would ensure roles are understood and any possible alterations/modifications during the performance can be made and changes agreed afterwards if necessary.
	Negative impact on performance
	Lack of communication within a team or group performance would mean confusion could occur. Roles might not be clearly explained or understood. Performers might then do the wrong thing, move to the wrong place or mark the wrong person. This would leave someone unmarked, a dancer without their partner in the correct place to complete an assisted lift or an opponent with a clear shot at goal because a player did not cover the required area of the goal.

Check your progress

	HELP NEEDED	*GETTING THERE*	*CONFIDENT*
1. Describe how the mental factor might influence a dancer who suddenly becomes aware of the audience during an important display.			

Advice from marker – try to use your knowledge from activities you are familiar with which can also be affected by a crowd, supporters or an audience.

	HELP NEEDED	*GETTING THERE*	*CONFIDENT*
2. Describe how the physical factor might impact a performer's ability to sustain a consistent performance throughout a whole game, match, swim or routine.			

Advice from marker – you need to refer to what happens to skills and state of mind as tiredness begins to affect a performance.

	HELP NEEDED	*GETTING THERE*	*CONFIDENT*
3. Explain the importance of carrying out duties or roles effectively before and during a performance.			

Advice from marker – give details about the roles which exist in a range of activities and explain how these things can influence your own and others' understanding about what is to be done while the performance takes place.

Data collection

4A Data collection

In this chapter you will learn:

1. Methods of data collection for all four factors – mental, emotional, social and physical.
2. How to carry out these methods.
3. To understand and evaluate the benefits and limitations of data collection.

In this section of the book you will identify, describe and review the methods of data collection. The table below highlights the methods you are going to address.

Factor	Method	Page number
Mental: mental state	POMS test	45
Mental: anticipation and mental toughness	Self-reflection profile	47
Emotional: anxiety	Scat test	49
Emotional: self-control and channeling aggression	Disciplinary record	52
Social: working in isolation	Team/Group feedback	55, 57
Social: gender issues	Personal reflection	56
Social: communication	Communication questionnaire	58
Physical: Aerobic endurance	Time-related observation schedule	60
Physical: anaerobic endurance	PaceTracker app	63
Physical: explosive power	Sargent Jump	65
Physical: consistency of skills	General observation schedule	67
Physical: consistency of sub-routines	Skill test	68
Physical: consistency of creativity	Self-assessment	71
Physical: role-related demands and team strengths and weaknesses – strategy, formation or composition	Feedback	73
Physical: role-related demands	Own or opponents' game analysis	74

What should I already know?

During the National 5 course, you will have carried out a variety of different data collection methods and explained why they were appropriate.

You will have been given many opportunities to gather information on different performances and used a range of different methods, such as video, tablets, observation schedules, informal discussions. Think back and try to remember what you have used and how you carried them out.

The Higher course will build on the skills and knowledge developed at National 5 level and lead to a more in-depth analysis of the methods of data collection and how they compare to each other.

Introduction to data collection – mandatory skills and knowledge

The 'mandatory skills and knowledge' required for this area are particularly concerned with:

- Your choice of methods
- The reliability and practicability of the methods chosen
- The protocols for setting out these methods
- The qualitative, quantitative, objective and subjective information the methods provide
- How the feedback (data you generate) is given to you.

This applies to all factors.

Let's look at each section separately before we go on to investigate the different methods of data collection for each factor.

Your choice of methods

You will have chosen the methods because they specifically test what you require them to test. However, if there is more than one method available you need to be able to justify why you chose one over the other or indeed used them both.

The reliability and practicability of the methods chosen

This will form part of your justification for using the methods you did. The methods you use must produce results that are reliable and therefore can be repeated again, post training, to allow for comparisons. Also they must be practical and able to be used in the activities of your choice. For example using speed gates to test speed in a swimming pool would not be possible.

The protocols (rules)

The protocols for organising and setting out these methods must be clear. This again enables the test to be repeated under the same conditions each time. This is a very important consideration in terms of generating reliable results.

The qualitative, quantitative, objective and subjective information the methods provide

This area relates to the type of information generated by the method of data collection. You must be able to show you understand if the information is factual and unbiased. This is likely to be results of a standardised test where there is little chance of error and where opinion – subjective data – is **not** involved. For example the results of the Sargent Jump test for power. A figure – quantitative data – is given. There is no subjective data involved. However when using the data generated from the general observation schedule, opinions – qualitative judgments – from an observer are simply recorded on the sheet. Even if you did this yourself using a recording of your performance, some opinion – subjectivity – might still be possible.

It is wise to be able to differentiate between each of the types of data collection and understand which are:

- Completely objective
- Partially objective
- Completely subjective
- Quantitative data
- Qualitative data.

Where possible a combination of quantitative, objective data with some qualitative information provides a good starting point for planning performance improvement. This is because it gives a wide, detailed picture of the whole performance.

By being aware of the issues relating to reliability, qualitative data can still be very useful. If you understand the data you collect has to be as **accurate** and **reliable** as possible then you will try hard to eliminate as much subjectivity (opinion) as possible. You can do this by getting two people to administer the observation schedule. One can write, the other can call out their observations. Details will therefore not be missed. You can also record the performance and get a teacher or coach to complete the analysis with you. This cuts down the risk of any judgments based on opinion or bias.

Skills for life, learning and work

Your success will always be measured in every walk of life. In school we are measured by the number of days we are absent, the number of clubs we attend, the number of exams we pass. It is useful to understand which are most important. Opinions (subjective and qualitative data) are often asked for from employers about one person's judgments about your suitability for a job for example. Objective data in the form of the number of absences you had or the number and level of qualifications you achieved are also of interest to further education institutes and employers.

Consider carefully the methods of data collection that follow and try to think about how much factual evidence and opinion they provide. This will help you understand the issues relating to reliability and suitability.

4B

Methods of data collection for the mental factor

Mental state: Profile of Mood Status (POMS), by McNair et al (1971)

A POMS allows you to gather information on your mental state during your performance. Collecting information on key mental features such as anger, frustration, concentration and tension will allow you to identify your own personal strengths and development needs in this factor. In this chapter, you will look at carrying out a POMS to collect data on **mental toughness**. A POMS can be completed as a paper or electronic questionnaire.

How to carry out a POMS

A teacher/coach/peer will ask you a series of questions after your performance relating to your mental state during your performance. These questions will be measured against statements such as Always, Occasionally, Never. At the end of the test, the recorder will analyse the results and present a score for each of the features by allocating marks for each answer. This can then be compared against national norms, which will allow you to determine where your strengths and development needs lie.

Activity 4.1

With a partner, research POMS tests online and find one that you can complete.

Analyse your responses, find your scores and then compare these scores against the norms.

Some examples are given below.

	Extent of feeling		
Feeling	**Always**	**Occasionally**	**Never**
Angry			
Tense			
On edge			
Grouchy			
Furious			

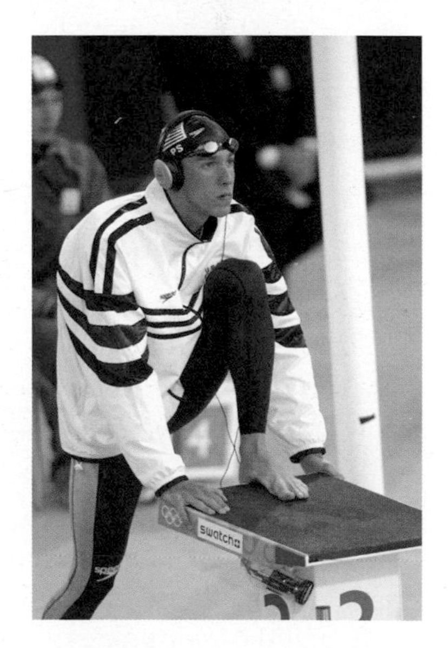

Make the Link

This method of data collection could also be used for some of the emotional factors that may impact your performance. It may be a useful method to consider how mental and emotional factors are interlinked when considering your performance development. This way you will be able to come up with a plan that will develop both factors.

Benefits of a POMS test

- Consistent questions increase the reliability of this test. Also, the format of the questions allows the performer to give direct responses, thereby aiding the reliability of the test.
- Easy and quick to use. The test can be accessed easily online, allowing the performer a quick means of gathering information on mental factors.
- The test is recognised, which increases the validity of the data collected.
- Comparison against norms. If the test is completed online, the performer will gain a quick analysis and score, which can be compared against national statistics.

Limitations of a POMS test

- As performers can only pick from the options given, the test may not consider the specific personal mental qualities of performers. Results may therefore be inaccurate.
- The test may hinder a performer's potential by labelling him/her with a particular strength or weakness.

Activity 4.2

Consider your own performance. Why not complete the POMS test after a practice for your course assessment single performance? For example, you may be completing your single performance in basketball. Complete the POMS test after a game situation. What information have you been able to gather from this test? What does this information tell you about your performance and how your mood can impact on your performance?

Skills for life, learning and work

The POMS test could be used in conjunction with many other aspects of your daily life, for example your studies or your clubs outside of school. Perhaps it will give you an insight into how your mental and emotional wellbeing can impact other key areas of your personal development, for example your own confidence and self-esteem or how you cope with leadership opportunities.

Anticipation and mental toughness: self-reflection profile

A self-reflection profile is a method you can use to gather information on the mental factor during your performance. The simple profile below allows you to gather information on a variety of features within the mental factor.

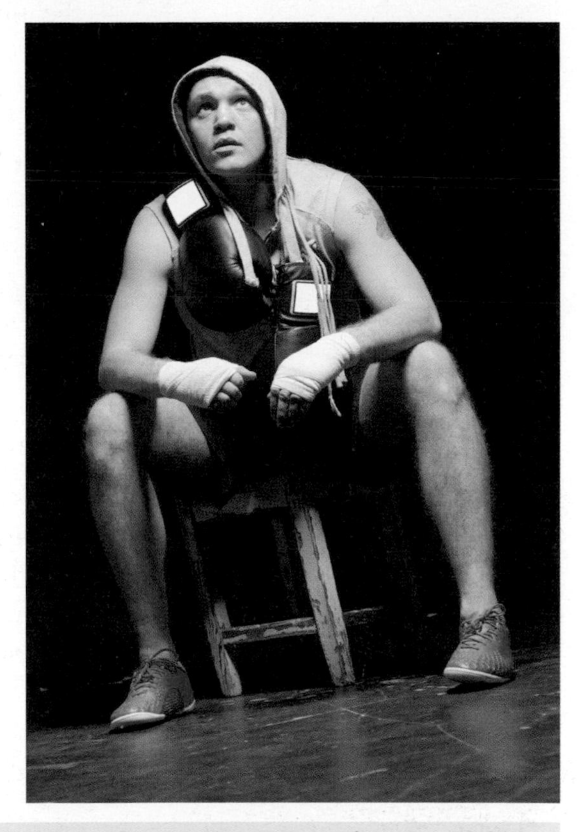

How to carry out a self-reflection profile

Take some time immediately after your performance to write up some reflective comments into a profile. Make sure you are in a quiet space so you can focus and consider some of the strengths and development needs you have identified previously. Read over your comments and perhaps share them with a classmate or teacher/coach.

The profile below is an example of one you may wish to use.

Mental feature	Comment
Mental toughness: Are you able to keep focused when faced with difficult situations in your performance? Are you able to keep calm when faced with difficult situations in your performance? Are you able to make effective decisions at crucial points in your performance? Can you cope when parts of your performance have not gone to plan?	
Anticipation: Are you able to respond to specific cues in your performance? Are you able to make the correct decisions relevant to the cues in your performance? Are you able to anticipate key performance demands in advance? Are you able to shorten the time you take when responding to a cue?	

Benefits of a self-reflection profile

- You are able to gather information from your own personal feelings on key questions in your performance.
- You can gather information on specific mental features. For example, the information in the preceding table clearly looks at key questions on mental toughness and anticipation. This way you are able to design your profile around the key features on which you wish to collect data, which increases the validity of this method.
- It is simple to carry out, as it does not require the involvement of anyone else.
- It is quick to carry out, as it can be completed in a reasonably short amount of time directly after your performance.

Limitations of a self-reflection profile

- When completing the profile, performers may elevate their comments to suit the performance, resulting in loss of reliability.
- The performer may feel they do not have enough experience or expertise to complete the test.
- Some performers may feel self-conscious about completing a profile on their own performance.

GO! Activity 4.3

Think through some of the mental features that may have an impact on your performance, such as problem solving, concentration or motivation. Design a self-reflection profile for an activity of your choice that focuses on these mental features.

4C Methods of data collection for the emotional factor

SCAT – Sports Competition Anxiety Test, by Martes, R. et al (1990) *Competitive Anxiety in Sport*

A SCAT allows you to analyse your responses to specific questions relating to how you feel emotionally during your performance.

How to carry out a SCAT

Normally your teacher/coach or peer will ask you a series of questions after a performance based on your emotional wellbeing during a performance. This can be completed on paper or online.

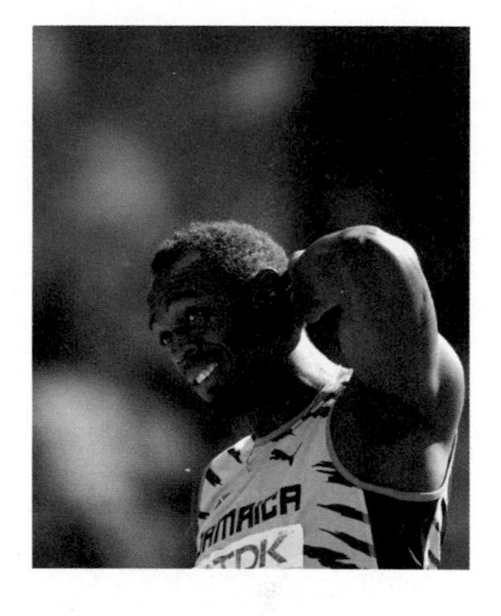

A series of questions will be posed – here are some examples:

- Do you feel relaxed before a performance?
- Do you become agitated before a performance?
- Do you feel nauseous before a performance?

Each question will allow you to respond from a drop-down menu, or the recorder will tick the appropriate term, e.g. Always, Occasionally, Never.

There are many online SCAT tests, e.g. http://www.brianmac.co.uk/scat.htm.

Activity 4.4

Use the following SCAT and ask an assistant to complete it for you.

Sport Competition Anxiety Test (SCAT)

Assessing Your Anxiety

Read each statement below. Decide if you 'rarely', 'sometimes', or 'often', feel this way when competing in your sport. Tick the appropriate box to indicate your response.

	Rarely	Sometimes	Often
1. Competing against others is socially enjoyable			
2. Before I compete I feel uneasy			
3. Before I compete I worry about not performing well			
4. I am a good sportsperson when I compete			
5. When I compete, I worry about mistakes			
6. Before I compete I am calm			
7. Setting a goal is important when competing			
8. Before I compete I get a queasy feeling in my stomach			
9. Just before competing, I notice my heart beats faster than usual			
10. I like to compete in games that demand a lot of physical energy			
11. Before I compete I feel relaxed			
12. Before I compete I feel nervous			
13. Team sports are more exciting than individual sports			
14. I get nervous waiting to start the game			
15. Before I compete I usually get uptight			

Athlete's name ______________________________

Analysis

The score for the response to each question is detailed below. Enter the score for each question in the 'Athlete's Score' column and then total the column up to provide a SCAT score.

Note that questions 1, 4, 7, 10 and 13 score zero regardless of the response.

Question	Rarely	Sometimes	Often	Athlete's Score
1	0	0	0	
2	1	2	3	
3	1	2	3	
4	0	0	0	
5	1	2	3	
6	3	2	1	
7	0	0	0	
8	1	2	3	
9	1	2	3	
10	0	0	0	
11	3	2	1	
12	1	2	3	
13	0	0	0	
14	1	2	3	
15	1	2	3	

Total SCAT Score ______

SCAT Score	Analysis
Less than 17	You have a low level of anxiety
17 to 24	You have an average level of anxiety
More than 24	You have a high level of anxiety

Benefits of a SCAT test

- The test is designed to measure **specific** emotions during your performance.
- Consistent set questions make it a reliable and accurate method, as the data cannot be misinterpreted. Also, the format of the questions allows the performer to give direct responses, thereby aiding the reliability of the test.
- Easy and quick to use. The test can be accessed easily online, allowing the performer a quick means of gathering information on mental factors.
- The test is recognised, which increases the validity of the data collected.
- Comparison against norms. If the test is completed online, the performer will gain a quick analysis and score, which can be compared against national statistics.
- You are able to compare your results from different performances. This will increase the reliability of your data.
- No equipment is required.

Limitations of a SCAT test

- In order to complete the test, performers need to be able to administer and understand the data, e.g. they must be able to make effective comparisons. If they do not do this properly, the results could lack validity.
- The test relies on the performer's ability to be strict with themselves when answering questions, therefore a de-motivated performer may not complete the test as reliably as a motivated performer.

Self-control and channelling aggression: disciplinary record

Most team and individual sports will have a method to record any disciplinary incidents that occur during performances. If a referee/umpire needs to take disciplinary action, they will normally have an immediate sanction at the time of the incident and a follow-up sanction after the performance. The sanction will be recorded during the performance by the referee/umpire and through the governing body.

A disciplinary record can also give the performer a method of gathering information on their emotional conduct throughout their performances. It will allow the performer to gather a picture of how their emotions have impacted on their performances and compare their emotions in different performances.

Below is an example of a disciplinary record.

Player	Club	Incident	Sanction	Sanction
R Leckie	Hamilton Hawks	Deliberate foul Lost control of emotions after losing possession of the ball an opponent.	Removed from game	3 week game ban
S Mitchell	Carnoustie Cougars	Used abusive language and became aggressive towards umpire when a foul was called.	Personal foul added Removed from court	Disciplinary meeting with governing body

MISCONDUCT REPORT FORM

TO: ....
....
....

Match .... Date of Match ....
Venue .... Competition ....
Player Reported .... Club ....

Send Off/Cautionable .... Number Worn By Player ..... Time of Offence ....

- Enter the offence as shown below e.g. A1, B2.

A. Sending Off Offences

1. is guilty of serious foul Play
2. is guilty of violent play
3. spits at an opponent or other person
4. denies a goal or a goal-scoring opportunity deliberately handling the ball
5. denies a goal or a goal-scoring opportunity by other means
6. uses offensive, insulting or abusive language
7. **receives a second caution**

B. Cautionable Offences

1. is guilty of unsporting behaviour
2. dissents by word or action
3. persistently infringes the Laws of the game
4. delays the restart of play
5. fails to respect the required distance at the taking of a corner kick or free kick
6. enters the field of play without permission
7. leaves the field of play without permission

The incident occurred as follows :

....
....
....
....

The player was informed that he was being *cautioned/sent off and that the matter would be reported to the appropriate association.

Signed .... * Referee /Assist. Referee
S.F.A. Registration No .... Name ....
Association: ....

Date ....

* Delete as appropriate
- ❑ This copy to be in the Secretary's hands no later than 3rd day following the match.
- ❑ One copy to be retained by Referee

How to carry out a disciplinary record

The performer should be given an opportunity to look over any disciplinary records and be aware of the impact they may be having on their performance. Through discussion and by sharing this information, they may be able to reflect on their own emotional performance and consider any apparent patterns of behaviour.

Benefits of a disciplinary record?

- The record enables the performer to self reflect and consider the impact their emotions are having on their performance.
- The discipline record will collect factual information, which both the player and their coach/teacher can use to develop approaches to help.
- The coach and governing body are able to keep track of a player's emotional well-being and potentially use this information when required.

Limitations of a disciplinary record

- Relies on the an accurate account being recorded by the official, to make sure that it is factually correct
- It can de-motivate the performer, who may not agree with the decisions that have been made

4D

Methods of data collection for the social factor

Group dynamics: team/group feedback

One of the most beneficial methods of gathering information would be to consider some team/group feedback. This can be highly effective when considering how positive 'group dynamics' are required during a performance and when you need to gather information on how your group works together.

Again, a simple feedback profile could be designed.

Social feature	Comment
During my performance how did I cope when working as part of a group? Did I communicate? Was I willing to listen? Did I accept others' opinions?	
During my performance, how did I cope when working in isolation? Was I able to focus? Was I confident in my own decisions? Was I concerned about what my teammates might think? Did I feel included in the overall performance?	

How to carry out team/group feedback

This method of collecting information on a specific feature can be used by the individual performer or by asking a coach/teacher/peer to pose the questions. It may also lead to some discussion between the performer and the coach/teacher/peer. It is best if this type of profile is completed directly after performance, so that key details are still fresh in the memory and the responses given are therefore accurate.

Benefits of team/group feedback

- This method is beneficial because it can focus on a range of features within this factor.
- It gives information to the performer about how various aspects of the social factor impact performance.
- By answering the questions honestly, an accurate picture of the group dynamics can be gathered. For example it might highlight that the girls feel they are being criticised by the male members of their team or group.
- This can be a good starting point when trying to identify an aspect of performance that needs to be tackled.
- As all members of the group would receive feedback, common areas for development can be agreed and taken forward.

Limitations of team/group feedback

- Performers may feel embarrassed being given feedback in front of other people and may prefer to receive feedback outwith the team/group. However, giving feedback to individuals, rather than the whole group/team, could undermine group cohesion.
- It may be difficult to pitch the feedback so that it is at the correct level and understood by all performers.

Gender issues: personal reflection

Reflecting on key social factors after a performance, such as gender issues, allows the performer to gather specific information on how these factors impacted on performance.

Below is the personal reflection of a performer after a basketball game:

During the class basketball competition, it became evident that many of the girls did not receive the ball, even when they were in space. Although the girls often tried to shout for the ball, the boys' decision was often to look for another boy to pass the ball to. This eventually resulted in a small number of girls opting out of the game, preferring to stand in isolation. I felt pulled between supporting the girls and trying to produce a good performance.

How to carry out a personal reflection

A personal reflection statement is written up or recorded directly after a performance. It can be completed on your own or in a group.

Benefits of personal reflection

- A personal reflection allows the performer to focus on specific social issues and how they have impacted on the performance.
- The personal reflection does not involve anyone else, therefore it is simple to complete.
- It allows the performer to write down their own personal thoughts without any pressure from others.

Limitations of personal reflection

- Personal reflection relies solely on individuals being truthful about their own performances. Performers may give invalid information to try to enhance their performances.
- Personal reflection relies on the subjective opinion of individuals.

GO! Activity 4.5

Consider a performance that you have taken part in recently. Copy out the box below and record in it any social features that may have had an impact either positively or negatively on your performance. Try to write an honest account of both your own performance and the performances of others in the group.

Personal Reflection Statement

Issues relating to working in isolation: method of data collection – coach feedback record

During your performance, your coach/teacher may be able to gather information on specific social factors that may have an impact on your performance. Your coach/teacher will write down comments as you perform and address these with you after the performance.

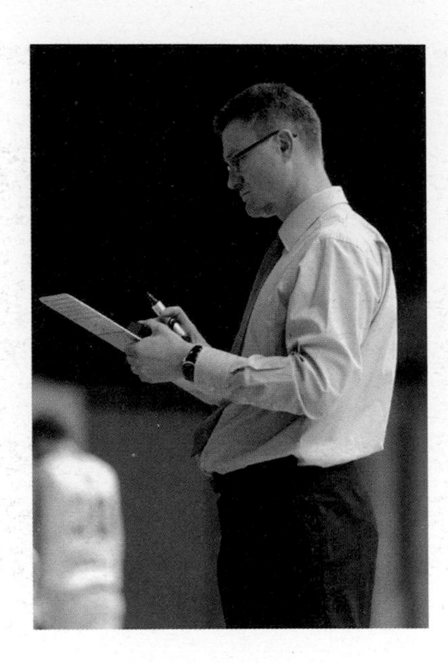

How to carry out a coach feedback record

During a performance, the coach will record how individuals carried out specific roles as they worked in isolation. They will then be able to make specific comments about how the performers met the demands relating to working on their own.

Benefits of coach feedback

- Feedback is written down immediately, which may help with the reliability of the information you have gathered.
- The coach/teacher then will have an opportunity to share the feedback with you, allowing a greater understanding of the key information. This will then allow the performer to consider their strengths and development needs.
- Communication between the coach/teacher and performer is a valuable mechanism to analyse information and to then decide on the best approaches for performance development.

Limitations of coach feedback

- If feedback cannot be given immediately after a performance, a coach's recollection of events may become inaccurate over time and reliable information may not be fed back to the performer.
- If feedback is being given during a performance, information may not be heard, especially in a team game situation.

Communication: communication questionnaire

Below is an example of some of the questions you may wish to ask in a questionnaire when trying to gather data on communication.

Questions	Yes	No	Examples
During performance do you use verbal communication?			
Is your communication clear, concise and correct?			
Do you use verbal communication to encourage?			
Are you positive when communicating?			
During your performance do you use non verbal communication?			
Is your non verbal communication clear, concise and correct?			
Do you use non verbal communication to encourage?			

How to carry out a communication questionnaire

After your performance, take some time to answer the questionnaire based on communication. You can do this by yourself or with a partner. Take some time to consider backing up your answers with some examples; this will allow the information gathered to be more reliable evidence.

Benefits of a questionnaire

- It allows the performer to devise the appropriate types of communication questions for the specific performance, whether a team/ group performance or individual.
- By having examples, the information gathered will be more concise and reliable.
- It can be completed by the performer, so that it is easily done straight after performance.
- It can be completed with a partner to allow further discussion.

Limitations of a questionnaire

- The performer needs to give honest responses if accurate data is to be collected.
- If the questionnaire is not completed directly after a performance, the performer may not give a reliable account of how they were feeling during the performance.

4E
Methods of data collection for the physical factor

Aerobic endurance: method of data collection – time-related observation schedule

A time-related observation schedule allows you to gather information on how your aerobic endurance can affect your performance. The example below is for a 20-minute basketball performance.

How to use a time-related observation schedule

During a 20-minute game, a classmate or a teacher/coach completes the time-related observation schedule or videos the performance so that the performer can watch it back and complete the schedule themselves. The teacher/coach must have a good view of the court and be able to focus completely on the task. It is important that the teams are of a similar standard so that the performance replicates a typical game.

The schedule on the next page concentrates on generating data for specific skill levels and movement patterns. The coach/teacher ticks when in the performance each level/pattern occurs, which can then be used by the performer to determine how their aerobic endurance impacts on their performance as the game progresses.

There is space at the bottom for the performer to include a brief analysis of the performance based on the data collected.

	Time in performance			
Skill level	0–5 mins	5–10 mins	10–15 mins	15–20 mins
Dribbling at speed				
Passing				
Set shot				
Lay up				
Jump shot				
Rebounding				
Receiving pass				
Movement patterns	0–5 mins	5–10 mins	10–15 mins	15–20 mins
Marking				
Moving into space quickly				
Tracking opponent at speed				
Movement in fast break				
Denying space				

✔ = effective
✖ = not effective

Summary of my strengths and development needs

Make the link

Consider other activities for which you would be able to gather information on how aerobic endurance impacts your performance. Perhaps you may already have some data on this factor.

Benefits of a time-related observation schedule

- Your performance can be tracked over a period of time to see how the length of the game can impact upon your aerobic endurance, in relation to the particular skills and movement patterns used.
- It allows you to gain information on specific time periods in your performance to see if there is a drop-off in performance in a certain area.
- It is quick and easy for a recorder to complete, which results in more accurate data.

Limitations of a time-related observation schedule

- If the performance is fast paced, it may be difficult to keep up and collect all of the information on the schedule. Vital data may be missed and feedback may not accurately reflect the performance.
- It can be time consuming to complete, especially if there are many performers each requiring individual information on their performance across a game. This may lead to the schedule not being completed in its entirety and vital information being missed.

Anaerobic endurance

Anaerobic endurance is the term used when the body is using oxygen quicker than it can be provided. This means that a different energy system has to be used in order to provide enough 'fuel' for the working muscles. When we are working anaerobically, we are effectively working without oxygen. The main source of 'fuel' comes from substances like glycogen that are stored in the body's cells. The main side effect of using this energy system is that a waste product called lactic acid gathers in the working muscles causing stiffness and soreness. Data collection for this area would look at **when** in a performance short sprints could no longer be reproduced.

Anaerobic endurance: PaceTracker app

There are many apps that allow the performer to gather information on a particular feature of the physical factor. For example, the PaceTracker app below takes you through a series of stages to collect data on your anaerobic endurance for a particular activity.

Using the PaceTracker app

The app takes you through the following process:

1. Choose a player or add a new player – type in the name of a player.
2. Select your court or pitch, check the dimensions and set a smaller or larger playing area if necessary.
3. Observer tracks your player using the app. Every place the player moves to is matched by moving the finger to the area on the playing area on the app.
4. A detailed analysis of the session is gathered including the average distance covered and average speed for the whole session. These can be presented in a graph or in figures.
5. Compares different sessions and allows comparisons and progress checks.

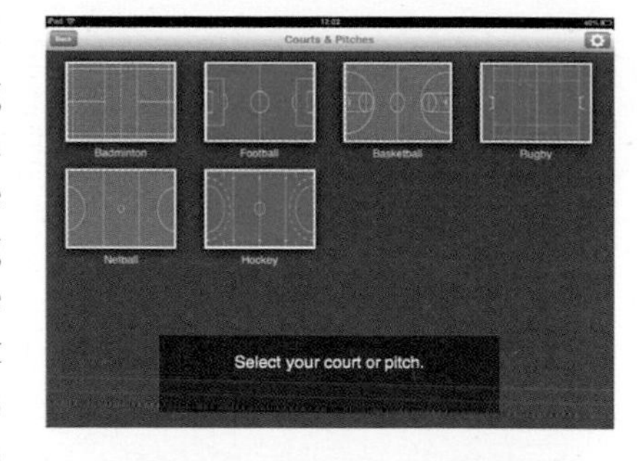

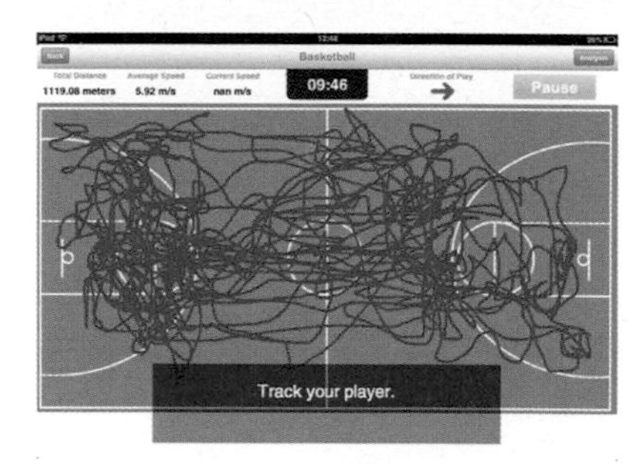

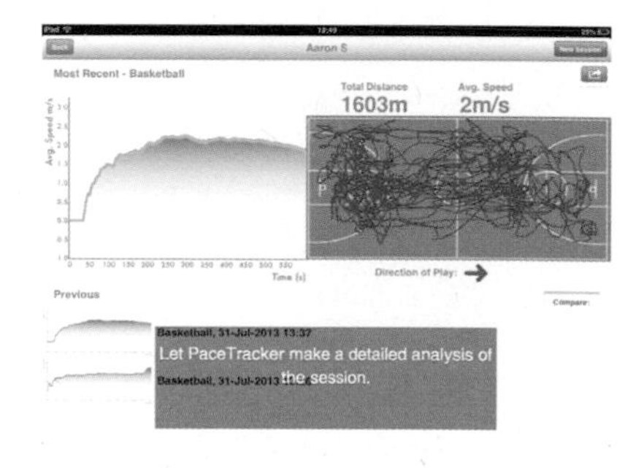

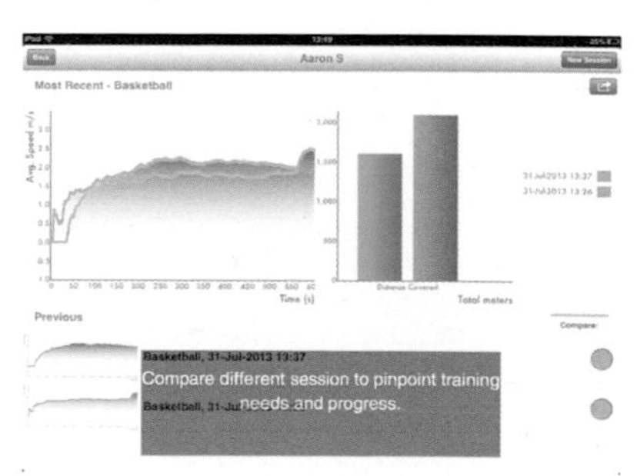

Benefits of PaceTracker app

- It gathers information and creates a detailed analysis. This allows a more robust and valid analysis, as the observer records directly into the app, which then completes an analysis.
- This can be stored on a tablet for later analysis and comparison.
- The performer gains specific objective, quantitative information that, by identifying objective distances and speeds produced in the game, will help them in their performance development.
- It is very simple to use and can be used in or outdoors.
- Results can be emailed to the performer to use as part of an overall analysis of performance before and after training.
- Due to the increasing popularity of mobile devices, many performers have access to this kind of data collection app.

Limitations of PaceTracker app

- It is dependent on individuals having access to a mobile device.

GO! **Activity 4.6**

Take some time to research the types of apps that are available. Make a list showing what is available and what they can be used for.
You can identify patterns in relation to the stage/time of the game.

Apps	Used
1.	
2.	
3.	
4	

Explosive power – Sargent Jump Test

Explosive power can impact a performer's ability to exert maximum force as quickly as possible. A variety of performers will require explosive power – for sprinting, bounding, kicking, pushing and hitting.

The aim of the Sargent Test Jump is to measure a performer's dynamic power (combination of strength and speed).

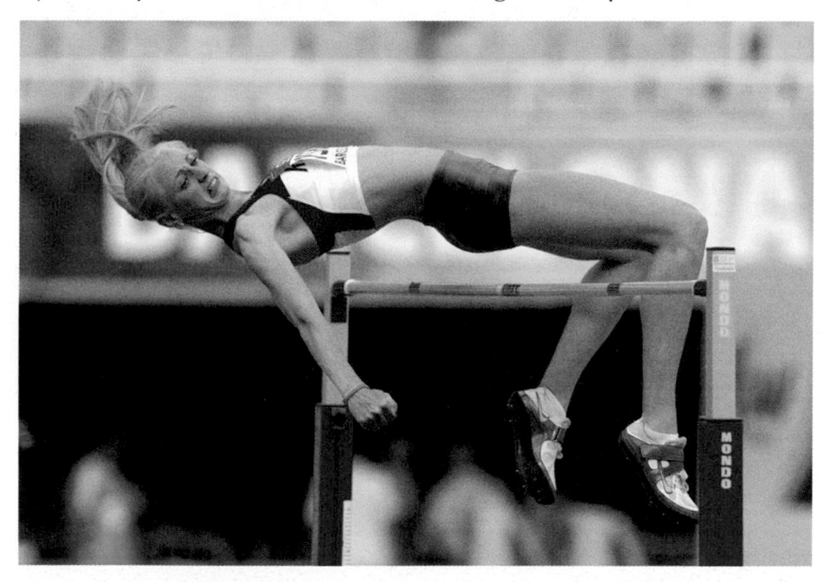

How to carry out a Sargent Jump

You will require a ladder, tape measure, steps, chalk and someone to assist you with the test. Your school may have a Sargent Jump board that you can use.

Make sure you have completed an appropriate warm-up, then complete the following stages:

1. Stand side on to the wall.
2. Extend your inside arm up against the wall.
3. Get a classmate to place a chalk mark on the wall at the tips of your fingers.
4. Rub some chalk onto your fingertips.
5. Still standing side on, bend down and jump upwards, as high as you can, marking the wall with your fingers.
6. Your classmate should record the distance between your first mark when standing and the second mark while jumping.
7. Complete this three times.
8. Take an average of the three attempts.

Record your score and use the following norms data table to compare against other performers for your age and gender.

The following are national norms for 15 to 19 year olds.

Gender	Excellent	Above average	Average	Below average	Poor
Male	> 65 cm	50 – 65 cm	40 – 49 cm	30 – 39 cm	< 30 cm
Female	> 58 cm	47 – 58 cm	36 – 46 cm	26 – 35 cm	< 26 cm

Benefits of the Sargent Jump Test

- The test offers a consistent mechanism to gather data on the leg power of a performer, which produces reliable results if completed correctly.
- The test is simple and quick to conduct.
- Making comparisons between performers is simple, as scores and national averages are available.
- Carried out indoors, therefore environment is controlled.

Limitations of the Sargent Jump Test

- All performers must complete the test under identical conditions. If they do not, the results may not be valid or reliable.
- Mistakes can be made when recording information and analysing data, especially when making comparisons to norms.

Consistency of skills – general observation schedule

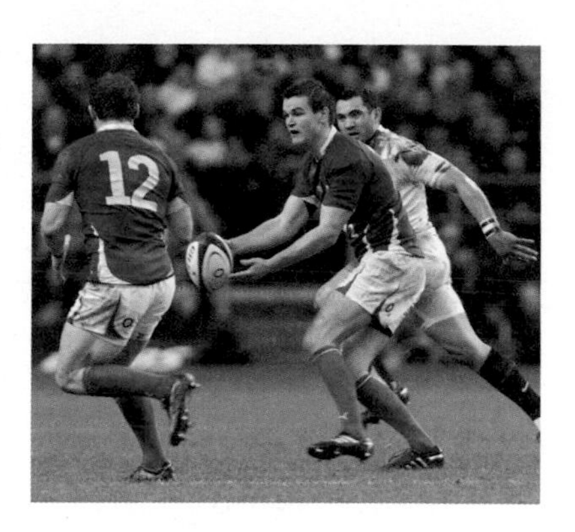

A general observation schedule allows you to design an observation method that will collect data on specific areas of your performance. There are many different kinds of general observation schedules: some will look at every area of your 'skilled' performance, whereas others will target specific areas.

A rugby player who wants to look at his consistency levels across three key skills – passing, receiving and tackling – may produce the general observation schedule below.

Method of data collection – general observation schedule

Skills observed – passing, receiving and tackling

Skill	Consistency	
	Met target	Off target
Pass 1		
Pass 2		
Pass 3		

Skill	Consistency	
	Received pass	Did not receive pass
Receiving pass 1		
Receiving pass 2		
Receiving pass 3		

Skill	Consistency	
	Successful tackle	Unsuccessful tackle
Tackle 1		
Tackle 2		
Tackle 3		

How to complete the general observation schedule

During a small game or a specific practice, an observer will record each time the performer passes, receives or tackles, by placing a tick in the appropriate box.

At the end, the performer can look back over the data to see how consistent he has been when using these skills.

Benefits of a general observation schedule

- Observation schedules allow a performer to gather information on a specific feature of their performance. The example above is collecting data on consistency.
- The information can be gathered easily, as there are specific skills to collect information on and the observer simply needs to note whether the skill has been successful or not.
- This could then be followed up in a detailed analysis.

Limitations of a general observation schedule

- If the performance is fast paced, it may be difficult to keep up and collect all of the information on the schedule. Vital data may be missed and feedback may not accurately reflect the performance.
- It can be time consuming to complete, especially if there are many performers each requiring individual information on their performance across a game. This may lead to the schedule not being completed in its entirety and vital information being missed.
- If the observer is susceptible to bias, then the reliability and validity of the information collected could be questioned.

Consistency of sub-routines: skill test

Skills testing can be specifically designed to gather information on the consistency of particular sub-routines of a skill.

The skill test below has been set up to gather information on the consistency of passing.

How to carry out a skill test

The working player has to execute 10 continuous passes by touching the line between the cones and turning and taking a pass from Blue 1 and passing to Blue 2.

Each pass is then measured against clear criteria and a point allocated for each criterion met. A recorder will keep a tally of the points.

Benefits of a skills test

- The test can be designed to suit your activity and your role within that activity.
- It will give you measurable information on how your performance development is progressing for the skill.
- The test can be designed to look at specific aspects of the skill, such as accuracy and consistency, which increases the validity of the information gathered.

Limitations of a skills test

- All performers must complete the test under identical conditions. If they do not, the results may not be valid or reliable.
- Mistakes can be made when recording information and analysing data, especially when making comparisons to norms.

SPORT EDU COACH SERVICES - RUGBY

Activity		*PASSING TEST*		Drill	*PIVOT PASSING*		
Equipment				Drill Requirement			
Balls	1	Bags	NA	Area	5 x 5 m		
Cones	4	Suits	NA	Players	3		
Shields	NA	Bags	NA	Time	NA		
Activity Description							
• Working player is required to execute 10 continuous passes by touching the line between the cones and turning and taking a pass from Blue 1 and passing to B2				Test will gather information on consistency of passing			

Set Up Diagram

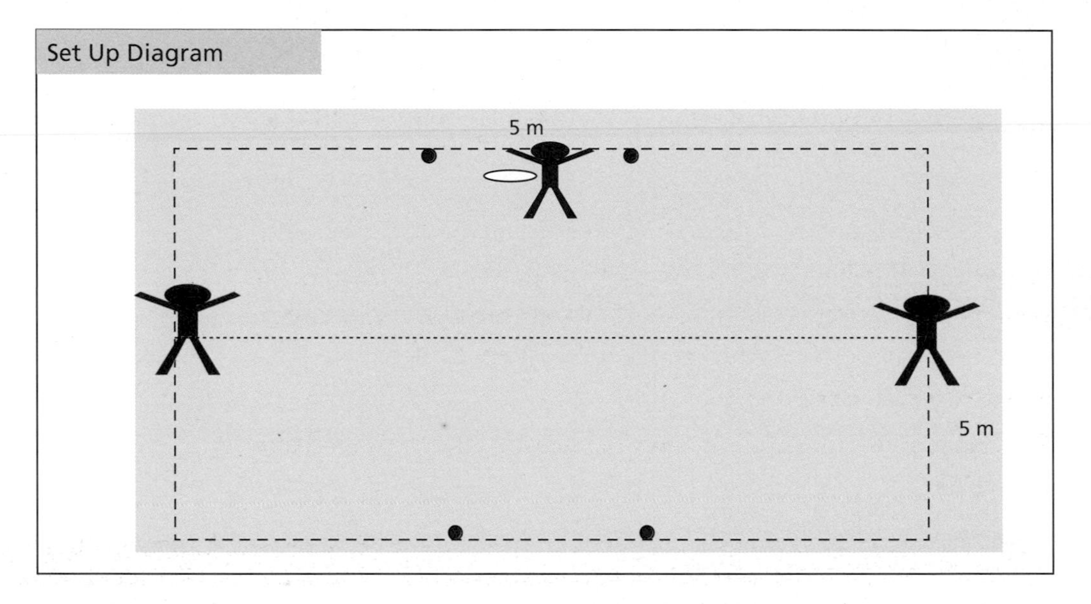

Key passing criteria	Scoring
1. Player must make a clean hand catch (no readjustment) 2. Player must catch the ball fingers pointing up 3. Player must execute a pass to the hands of the receiver (receiver may move hands to catch ball but cannot move feet)	Player receives a point for each success criteria Recorder keeps a tally of points scored

Activity 4.7

Design a skills test that will measure consistency and fluency in an activity of your choice.

Creativity: self-assessment

When gathering data on whether you have been creative in your performance, you may wish to consider completing a creativity self-assessment. An example is given below.

Creativity self-assessment

Top questions to ask on how creative you are in your performance

	Never	Sometimes	Always
I have good background knowledge of my activity			
I am curious during my performance			
I have good creative memory during my performance			
I can select a variety of skills to use			
I am happy to take risks during my performance			
I am patient during my performance			
I am not scared of failing			
I use my intuition			
I like to trust my gut instinct			
I use my imagination			
I can modify and adapt			
I am resilient			
I persevere			

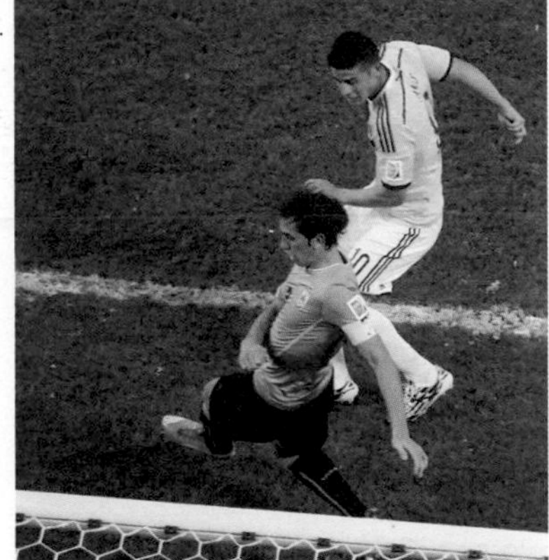

How to carry out the creativity self-assessment

Take some time to reflect on your past performances. Use the questions on the previous page as a stimulus to gather information on how creative you are. List your top three strengths and top two development needs from the self assessment.

Strengths	Development needs
1 ______________________	1 ______________________
2 ______________________	2 ______________________
3 ______________________	

Benefits of self-assessment

- It will allow you to take some time to consider the main aspects of Creativity in your performance.
- The questions draw out the types of skills required to be creative in your performance, allowing for more data.
- It can be completed in your own time.

Limitations of self-assessment

- Self-assessment relies solely on the individual being truthful about their own performance. Performers may give invalid information to try to enhance their performances.
- Self-assessment relies on the subjective opinion of individuals.

Role-related demands and team strengths and weaknesses – Strategy, formation and/or composition: feedback

Feedback on role-related demands within a strategy, formation/composition is one of the most common methods of gathering data when considering tactics and the choreographic devices required in aesthetic activities.

Receiving accurate and precise feedback on a performance is a highly effective method of gathering information. Outlined below is an example of feedback a dance teacher gave two performers on their duet dance routine, highlighting the specific roles they were performing.

Specific roles in performance	Comments for dance performer 1	Comments for dance performer 2
Performer 1 • Use of floor space • Strong/dynamic movements • Mirroring	You did not cover the whole floor when you carried out the triplet travelling sequence. You generally made the movements look strong, confident and dynamic. When mirroring, the level of your arm was slightly lower then your partner's.	
Performer 2 • Use of floor space • Soft/gentle movements		You did well getting from one corner of the stage to the other and you covered the floor well. Your movements were in keeping with the flow of the dance and looked gentle, flowing and elegant.

How was the feedback method carried out?

During the dance routine, the performers were given specific roles to carry out. Throughout the performance, the teacher was able to make specific comments on how the performers met the demands of their roles.

After the performance, a discussion took place about the strengths and development needs of their own particular roles and also how they were able to work together.

Benefits of feedback

- Feedback can be given immediately, so performers don't have to wait to receive an initial impression of their performance.
- Feedback can highlight the positives and negatives of a performance, which means constructive advice can be given on how best to improve performance.

Limitations of feedback

- If feedback cannot be given immediately after a performance, a coach's recollection of events may become inaccurate over time and reliable information may not be fed back to the performer.
- If feedback is being given during a performance, information may not be heard, especially in a team game situation.

Role-related demands – own or opponents' game analysis

During a performance, your coach/manager will seek to gather information on the role-related demands of your opponents. A match analysis will allow you, your coach and team to identify and gather specific information on the different principles of attack and defence that your opponents use.

How to carry out an opponents' game analysis

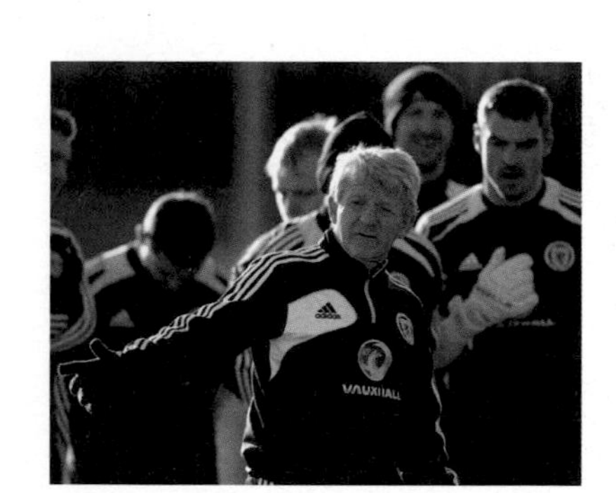

Players/coach/manager should have the opportunity to gather information on opponents and be able to give feedback to their team or an individual.

During a pre-planned performance, the coach/manager could gather information on opponents. This may take the form of a simple game analysis, where the coach/manager gathers information on specific tactics. This information would then be shared with the team or an individual on how best to exploit the opponents' performance.

Name of team:

Date of game:

Venue:

	4-4-2
	Comment
Depth	
Width	
Mobility	
Support	
Delay	

Benefits of a game analysis

- The analysis allows both the coach and the performer an opportunity to discuss the findings, which will allow them to come up with a plan.
- The coach and performer are able to dictate exactly what they are looking for in the performance, as they will set up the different situations on which they want to gather information.

Limitations of a game analysis

- If the performance is fast paced, it may be difficult to keep up and collect all of the information on the schedule. Vital data may be missed and feedback may not accurately reflect the performance.
- It can be time consuming to complete, especially if there are many performers each requiring individual information on their performance across a game. This may lead to the schedule not being completed in its entirety and vital information being missed.
- If the observer is susceptible to bias, then the reliability and validity of the information collected could be questioned.
- The 'observer effect' – when a performer is influenced by the presence of an observer – this may result in a performer changing their behaviour during an observation.
- Practicality – it is a resource intensive method. It requires the correct facilities and a number of performers.

4F
Data collection methods: summary

Why might you use different data collection methods?

The previous pages have given you descriptions and explanations of how to gather data on your performance, why the methods are useful and the merits of using different data collection methods. It is important that you are able to consider which methods best suit your activity, the factor or factors you are gathering information on and the type of performance context you will applying these methods to.

The table below outlines how you might decide which method to use.

Activity	Factor/feature	Method of data collection	Why?
Football	Mental – state	POMS test	This test is a **recognised** test, which is used across all sports. It will specifically give you information on mental awareness during a game of football. It will then give you a score, which can be used for comparisons at a later date.
	Social	Group feedback	Gathering feedback from peers and teachers/coaches can give you an **honest** picture of how you are performing socially during a football performance.
	Emotional – self control	Disciplinary record	This will allow you to have a permanent record of the types of behaviours that will have an impact on your performance. The record will be kept permanently allowing your coach and officials to look back at your performance and try to gather information on any emotional trends.

Dance	Physical – communication 	Communication questionnaire	You will be able to gain a **personal insight** into how communication has impacted on your group performance.
Tennis	Physical – skill 	Skills test	You will be able to gather **exact detail** on where and why the skill is breaking down. You can design the skills test to look at specific aspects such as consistency and fluency etc.
Hockey	Physical – fitness 	PaceTracker app	The PaceTracker app can be **easily used** in any facility. It will specifically track your speed over the period of your hockey game. It will then be able to give you a detailed analysis of the types of movement used during the duration of the game. It also gives a total distance covered in an entire match.

(*continued*)

Making comparisons of different data collection methods

You may have the opportunity to use a variety of different methods to gather information on factors that impact on your performance. The table on the next page highlights some examples and why it may be useful to use them together.

Activity	Factor	Methods	How were they used?	Comparison of both methods	Advantages and disadvantages of methods
Basketball	Physical – tactics – fast break	Game analysis Coach feedback	During a basketball performance, the coach gathered information by using a game analysis of the fast break and coach feedback.	By collecting information from two sources, I was adding to the validity and reliability of the data collected. The game analysis will help me gather information on the different aspects of the fast break during my game. Receiving feedback from our coach gave immediate feedback when the fast break broke down and what went wrong. Both methods will allow me to achieve an accurate picture of the strengths and weaknesses associated with the fast break.	The advantages of using a game analysis compared to coach feedback is that you will have objective data, which will be accurate and allow you to highlight the key areas of your performance that require development. Coach feedback will give you subjective information, which is based around the opinion of your coach/teacher. However, coach feedback allows you to discuss the opinions and come up with key suggestions as to how you are going to develop.
Trampoline	Emotional – fear Physical – skill	POMS General observation schedule	During my trampoline performance, I used a POMS to gather information on my anxiety levels and a general observation schedule to gather information on the range of skills completed.	Using these methods of data collection allowed me to highlight where in my performance I became anxious and the impact this had on my skill level. By using this combined approach, I was able to compare the data and then plan my development around my key needs.	The advantage of the POMS test is that it is a recognised test that can be easily completed online by the performer, who can then receive direct results and comparisons. As the test has been designed to highlight specific areas, it will be more reliable in obtaining the information. The general observation schedule requires someone to complete the observation schedule for you, which can lead to some mistakes being made. However you can design the general observation schedule specifically to your needs and what exactly you want to look at, making it more specific to your actual performance.
Badminton (Doubles)	Mental – concentra-tion Social – working as a team	Self-reflection profile Coach feedback	In my doubles badminton performance, I completed a self-reflection profile that highlighted the key areas in the game when I began to lose focus and concentration. At the same time, I received feedback from my coach about how well I was communicating and supporting my partner.	By comparing both of these methods, I can see that my lack of concentration is impacting my working partnership with my teammate. The profile clearly shows the parts of my game where I did not focus and this is directly linked to my lack of communication and support of my doubles partner. By using both of the methods I can see there is a clear correlation between my mental performance and how I am performing socially.	Both these methods offer a subjective opinion of whether a performance has been successful or not. Therefore both can be open to misrepresentation. However both offer opportunities to reflect upon the key areas of the performance and allow opportunities for discussion with others.

Check your progress

	HELP NEEDED	GETTING THERE	CONFIDENT
1. Explain the importance of the information a disciplinary record or a POMs analysis could give a coach when planning to organise a team for a crucial game.			

Advice from marker – Examine to what extent a coach might need her players to be in control, in terms of control of their emotions for a big game. Then add detail about what information a disciplinary record or POMs analysis would hold and explain how this would help the coach make decisions about the suitability for players to handle themselves appropriately when under pressure.

	HELP NEEDED	GETTING THERE	CONFIDENT
2. Describe one method of data collection for the social factor.			

Advice from marker – Give details about what the method looks like, what equipment is needed, where and when the test would be done.

	HELP NEEDED	GETTING THERE	CONFIDENT
3. Explain the differences between objective and subjective data.			

Advice from marker – Offer reasons why one type is different from the other and clarify what one type of data provides as compared to the other.

	HELP NEEDED	GETTING THERE	CONFIDENT
4. Evaluate the usefulness of using a video alongside an observation schedule.			

Advice from marker – Evaluate means explain the value and usefulness of being able to use a video as the observation is carried out. Is your analysis now more reliable? Is your data now more accurate? Was it easier to see what was happening in the performance recording?

	HELP NEEDED	GETTING THERE	CONFIDENT
5. Describe the feedback one method of data collection gave you about your whole performance.			

Advice from marker – Give details about areas that were development needs and also those that were strengths.

	HELP NEEDED	GETTING THERE	CONFIDENT
6. Explain why it is important to analyse a whole team's/group's performance when we are investigating the impact of gender issues on performance.			

Advice from marker – Develop your answer to show how an individual's strengths and development needs impact the needs of the whole group.

	HELP NEEDED	GETTING THERE	CONFIDENT
7. Describe the results of the comparison between your first and second PaceTracker analysis.			

Advice from marker – Take each piece of evidence generated, e.g. the total distance you covered in the match, the area of the court you covered, your average speed for the two performances, and show what differences there were and how this would have impacted on your ability to carry out your role within the performance.

Virgin
SHA
GLASGOW 2
XX COMMONWEALTH

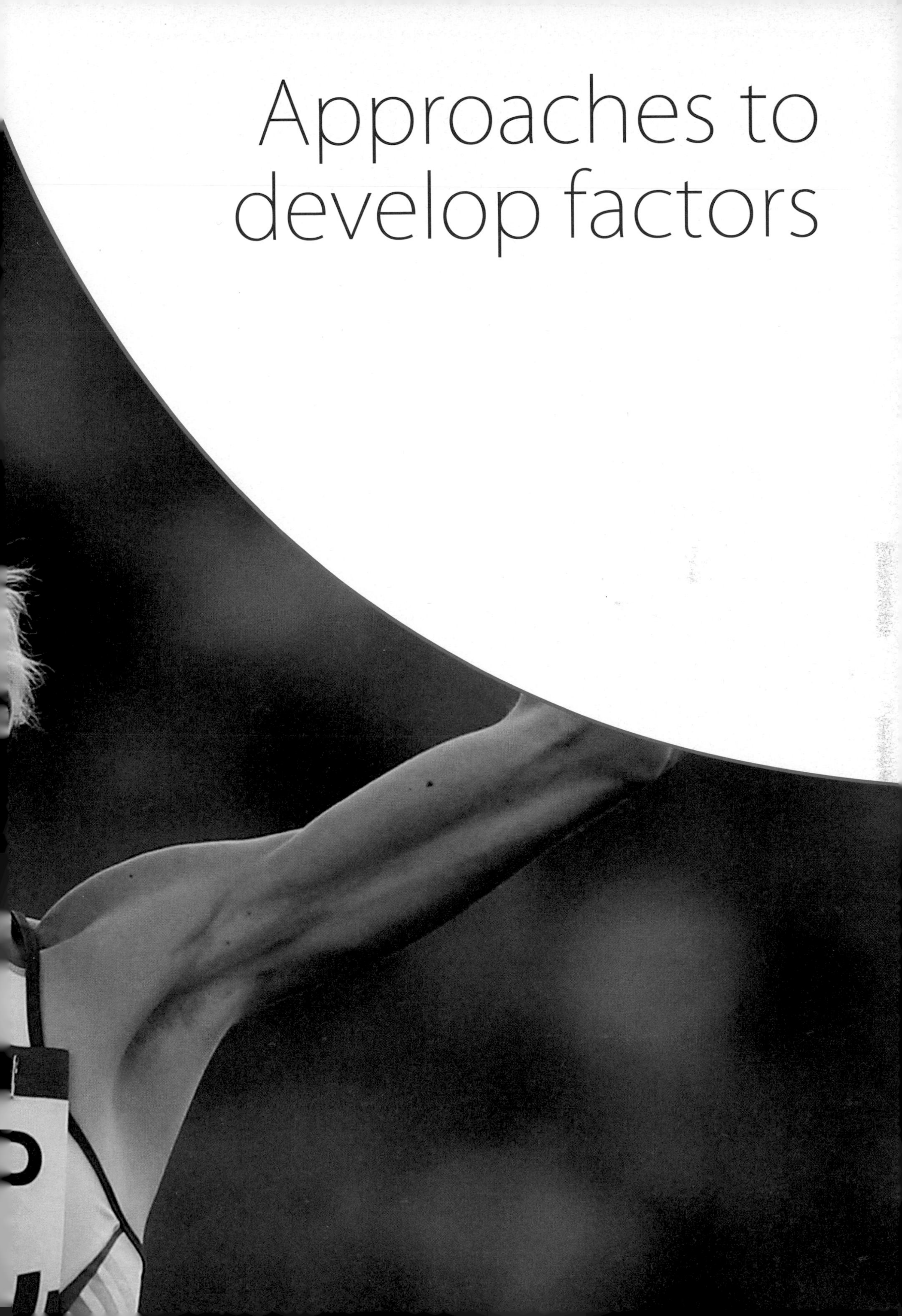

Approaches to develop factors

5 Approaches to develop the mental factor

In this chapter you will learn:

1. How mental toughness and anticipation can impact performance.
2. To understand, apply and evaluate approaches to improve mental toughness and anticipation.

The mental factor relates to processes in your brain associated with thinking. These are called **cognitive** processes. The two features we will look at are:

- Mental toughness (MT)
- Anticipation.

What should I already know?

The mental factor is an area that you might have investigated at National 4 or 5. At this level you will have examined how mental features can impact performance. In the Higher course you will look at the above features and investigate how they may influence your performance in more than one activity. In this way you will deepen your understanding about the impact of this factor.

Mental toughness

Activity 5.1

For an inspiring example of mental toughness watch these clips:

http://www.youtube.com/watch?v=dZO1cKiuya4

Describe the challenges Davina McCall had to overcome when taking part in this event.

http://www.youtube.com/watch?v=64A_AJjj8M4

http://www.youtube.com/watch?v=2xIzuyjCcZk

Describe the mental toughness these runners demonstrate to encourage themselves to complete the races.

Clip 1

Clip 2

Clip 3

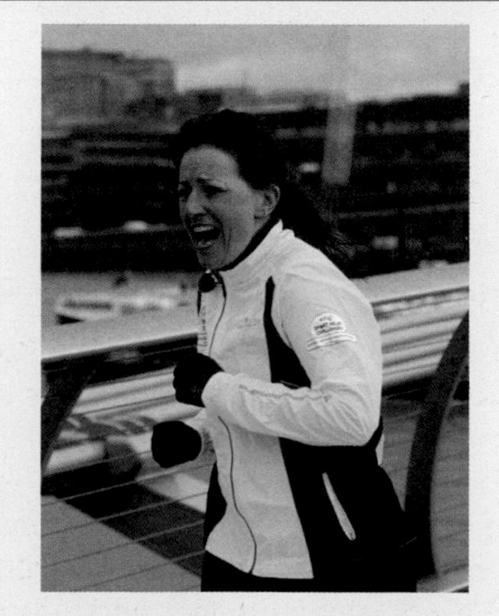

Mental toughness is very like resilience. You may have studied this feature when completing the National 4 or 5 courses. Resilience is the ability to keep going 'when the going gets tough'. Mental toughness is having a mindset that means you are prepared to deal with the difficulties a performance might bring.

To summarise, resilience is a positive process performers go through to recover from setbacks. Mental toughness is having the skills to deal with setbacks confidently and consistently. **Resilience is about carrying on and mental toughness is about seeking to use setbacks to your own advantage and, despite the pressure, still 'produce the goods'.**

Interesting fact

John Isner demonstrated incredible mental toughness when he won the longest ever tennis match at the 2010 Wimbledon Championships. The match was played over two days and lasted 11 hours, 5 minutes. Isner beat opponent Nicolas Mahut with a final score of 6–4, 3–6, 6–7, 70–68.

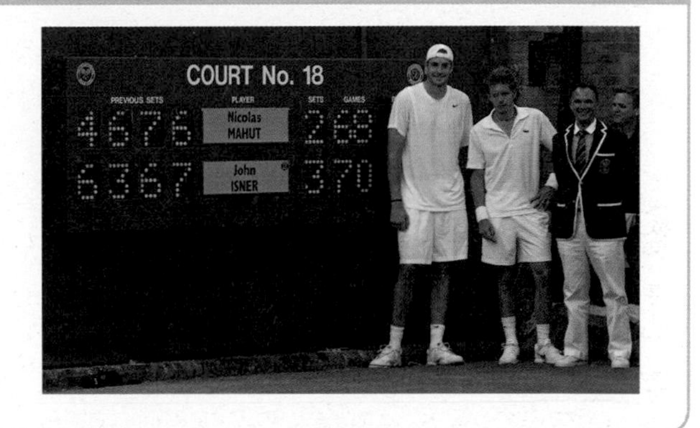

There has been a lot of research relating to mental toughness and how to enable performers to persevere both when under pressure and when a performance is going well. Having a high degree of MT allows you to cope with pressure, to handle failure and to push yourself to the limits required for success. Clough and Earle suggest there are four components to MT. These are:

- Confidence
- Challenge
- Control
- Commitment.

These are known as the **4 Cs**.

The approaches to develop mental toughness that we will look at in this book attempt to build these characteristics into a performer's mindset and thinking processes. Just as with any of the other factors, it would be very unusual for a performer to deal with only this one area of their performance. Rather, approaches to deal with MT are built into an overall development plan to improve the whole performance and the whole performer.

Psychological preparation

Tactical preparation

Technical preparation

Physical preparation

Mental toughness will enable you to develop the mental skills required to cope when you are faced with adversity. Resilience will ensure the performer recovers, but it is the MT that can mean the difference between success and failure.

MT is required whenever you feel uncomfortable. By becoming used to being outside your comfort zone when performing in practice, you will begin to familiarise yourself with the thoughts you experience when under pressure. This means that in the 'live' performance these thoughts will not be unfamiliar. You could think of it as developing your 'discomfort' zone. MT makes you more able to cope with the thoughts you have when in this zone. By becoming aware of **when** you start to feel uncomfortable, physically and or mentally, you are developing skills that enable you to identify exactly what it is in the performance environment that makes you feel uncomfortable. It could be:

- The presence of an audience or spectators
- Very good opposition/performers
- Feeling that you cannot control your own performance
- Feeling that you cannot win.

In many real-life situations mental toughness will be useful, especially when going for interviews, or completing tests and exams where you know you will be affected by the circumstances. Mental toughness should give you the skills to handle these pressures and feel confident you are able to succeed.

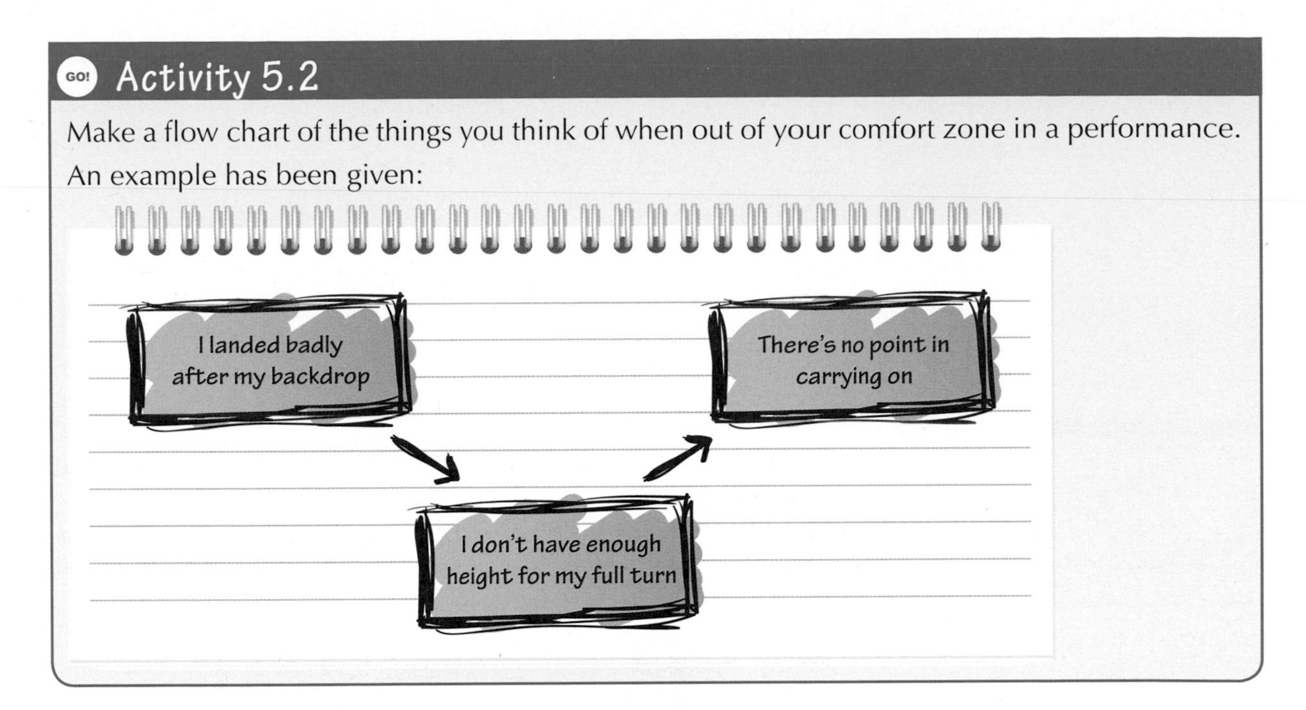

Approaches to develop mental toughness

Aversion training

A very simple approach you could use to deal with these feelings of 'discomfort' is '**aversion training**'. Basically, this means facing what you feel you can't deal with. This is the same type of approach you might use if you had a fear of flying or snakes!

In the performance environment the approach would be:

- Practise with an audience.
- Practise facing opposition stronger/better than you. Use self-control approaches to keep control of your emotions. While understanding and accepting that you will require resilience to accept things can go wrong, by staying focused and mentally tough you can recover from mistakes and go on to play your own game – even if you don't win.

Benefits of using this approach

It can be empowering to take control over your feelings. It is straightforward if you can get exposure to the type of challenge that is affecting your ability to remain mentally tough. Coping with feeling in control when you are out of your 'comfort zone' and feeling uncomfortable can also be an immensely positive thing.

Limitations of using this approach

Fear of failing, falling or making a fool of yourself can produce powerful emotions that can make you feel very weak. Asking a performer to put themselves in the position where they are being asked to face and deal with the very thing they find challenging is very difficult. It can only really be done over a period of time and with a great deal of support.

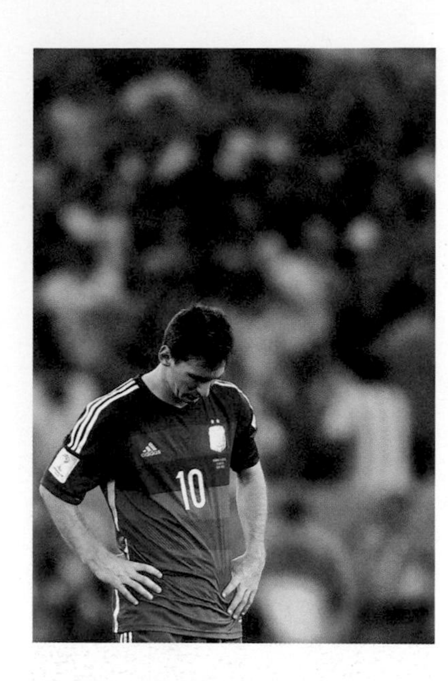

Reframing

A more structured approach to help develop MT is by '**reframing**'. This takes a performer through a process that involves changing negative thoughts, feelings or decisions into positive, task-orientated suggestions. The idea is that when something goes wrong, or you feel yourself slipping into the 'discomfort zone', you focus on a positive action that you can carry out to deal with the circumstances you find yourself in.

Here are some examples:

Example 1

'I'll never manage to score from this distance.'

Reframed thought would be – 'I'll push the ball high, aim just above the ring and move in quickly for any rebound.'

Example 2

'I'm not going to catch up with my opponent.'

Reframed thought would be – 'I'm going to close her down and put her under pressure.'

Example 3

'I can't remember what comes next.'

Reframed thought would be – 'I will carry on with this step and try to pick up what to do from the other dancers.'

This approach deliberately takes the thinking away from a mistake that has made the performer feel negatively about herself. In fact, it forces the performer to think:

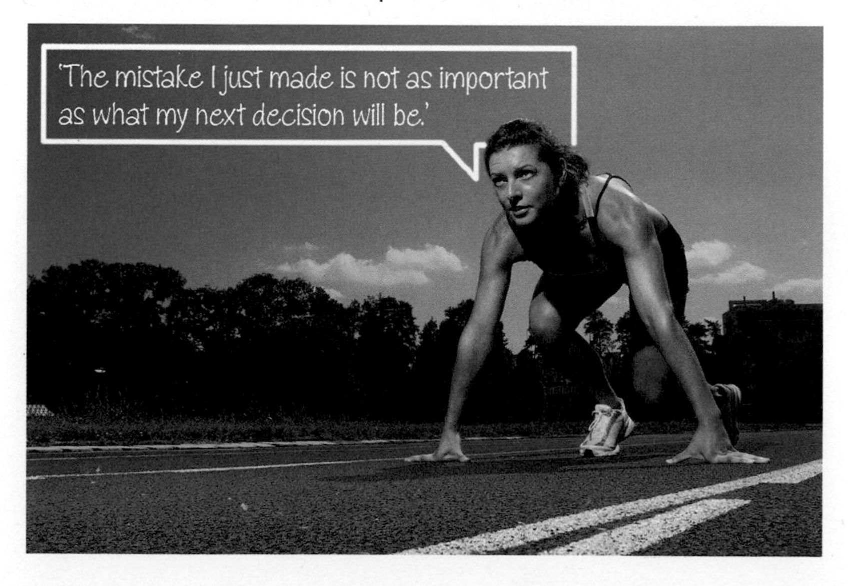

Reframing means just as its title suggests. A new frame is put around the next action that will be taken. It encourages the performer to stop thinking about what happened to trigger the feelings and instead to use MT to consider what she has to **do** to take charge of the performance situation. It is more than positive thinking – it is deliberately making the performer think about what to **do**, not just what to **think**. It does not ignore the problem but, as MT develops, it empowers the performer to focus on what she can control instead of the things that are outwith her control.

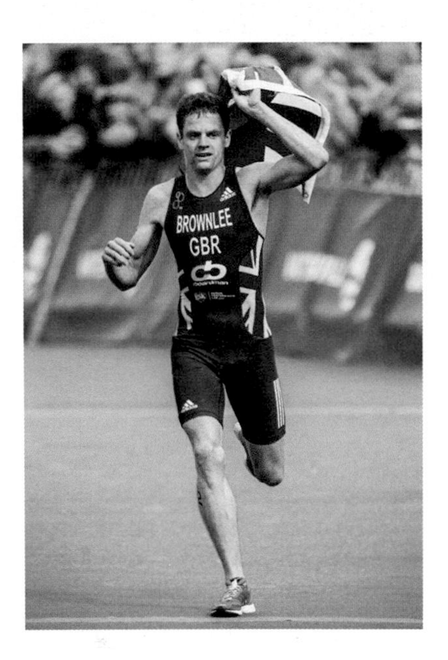

Benefits of using this approach

It is fairly straightforward to identify a positive element to any negative situation – with training. Learning can bring about the change of focus to enable a performer to find some positive aspect in even the most negative of situations. This approach can be used in many real life situations, from failing an exam to not getting a job you applied for.

Limitations of using this approach

Some people might say this is just another form of positive thinking and that there is simply one type of personality that views the glass as half full as opposed to half empty. Therefore, unless a performer is willing to really challenge the thought process they go through when they make a mistake, it is unlikely progress will be made.

 Assessment in PE

1.3 Explaining approaches to performance development based on these evaluations

By explaining why this approach is organised the way it is, you will achieve this assessment standard.

Learning how to use the reframing approach should be done in practice sessions. Prior to beginning the performance, the performer should think about what is involved. If at any point negativity begins to appear in this mental preparation, then she should immediately 'reframe' and think about **how** the dance starts, **which** foot she begins on or **where** she should stand before the centre pass is taken. Every thought should be about what she will **do**, not what she feels.

The performer should take part in rehearsals, races or games that replicate as near as possible the conditions of the final performance. However, as the performance progresses, attention should be given to when the performer begins to feel 'uncomfortable'. This signals the need for MT. If the performer senses that a challenge has come upon her that is too great, too difficult or too challenging, she must immediately think about what **course of action** she needs to take next. This might be:

- What position to take up
- What step to take
- Where to make the next pass
- When to resurface from a tumble turn
- With what skill to restart.

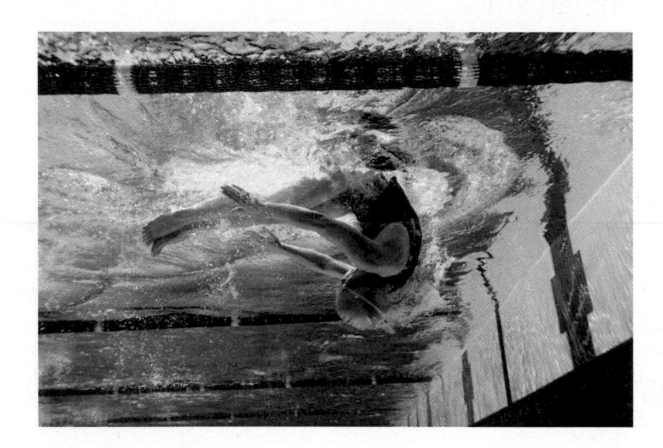

In effect, this 'reframing' approach makes use of thinking skills to encourage the performer not just to carry on (resilience) but also to maximise the likelihood that the **next** decision will be effective.

If you were to reframe a picture, then the picture would still be the same, but the frame in which it was held would be changed. In a performance context, 'reframing' means you will still have the same performance problem, but you will deal with it positively and constructively and so secure a positive outcome.

Assessment in PE

2.3 Implementing the development plan

By demonstrating the use of this approach as part of an overall development plan, you would achieve this assessment standard.

Success imagery

Another approach that can be beneficial when attempting to develop MT is 'success imagery'. As the name suggests, the performer has to project an image of success in the mind either before or during a performance in which they feel uncomfortable and require mental toughness.

This approach uses all the senses. These are:

- Smell
- Hearing
- Touch
- Taste
- Sight

The theory is that by becoming acutely aware of all of the signals the body is picking up from the senses, the image of the successful performance is easier to recall.

Performers need to develop an awareness of what a successful performance looks and feels like. If there are smells or tastes associated with this successful outcome then these too have to be considered and remembered. In a live performance situation it is unlikely these two senses will have much of a role to play in helping a performer who is using the success imagery approach. Nonetheless the smells associated with playing on a newly cut green when taking a winning putt or on the crease at cricket when batting to hold the lead in a tight match might add to the memories of a successful performance.

The process of using this approach is as follows:

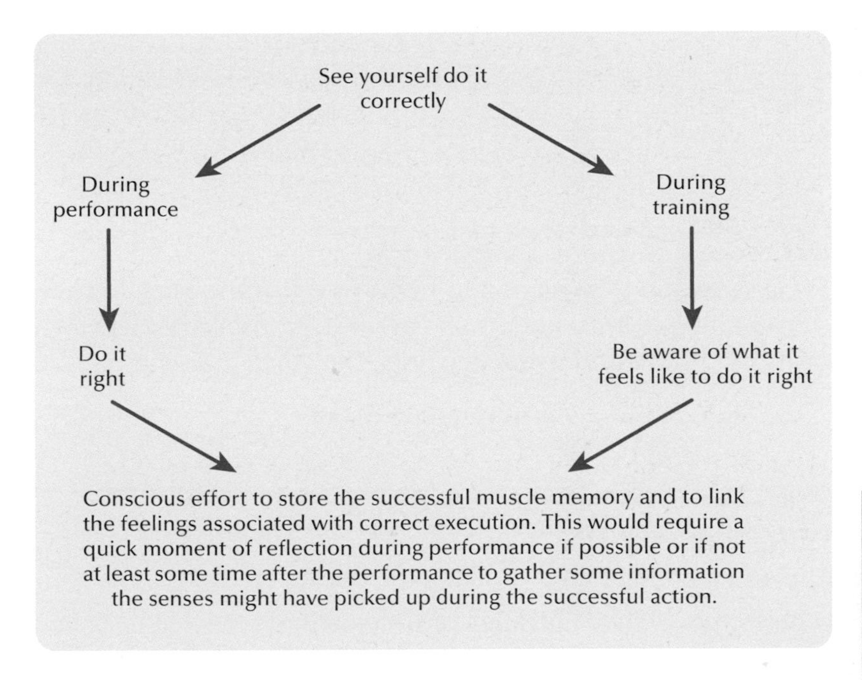

A rugby player practising conversion kicks in training would go through the process of seeing himself position the ball, look at the uprights, pace back the correct number of steps and then he would picture himself completing the kick perfectly. At the same time he would try to recall what sounds he would hear as the ball floated over the bar, what feelings he would have, what it felt like as his fellow players crowded around him. The more realistic and more detailed the imagery, the more likely MT will allow him to take control of the situation and complete the kick successfully.

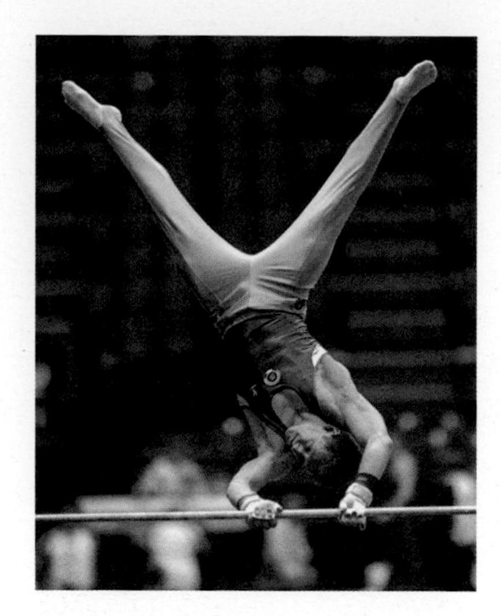

The gymnast would go through the same process. Each step of the routine would be replayed in the mind. The performer would experience the successful image of the routine being completed perfectly alongside the associated feelings, sights and sounds. This would be done after the routine had been completed.

Benefits of using this approach

In a stressful performance environment when MT is required, using the 'success imagery' approach can be a very powerful tool to ensure that the performer takes on challenges with confidence, commitment and control.

Remember, MT is not about **hoping** to recover from the possibilities of challenges, it is **knowing** that, **when** challenges come against you, you can not only recover and carry on (resilience), but can feel confident that you intend to overcome and succeed by taking on these challenges.

Mentally tough performers know for certain that challenges will come against them and they will not just overcome them but will use them to grow in confidence, knowing that by taking on the challenge they will be stronger and even more successful.

Limitations of using this approach

Success imagery requires the performer to be aware of their surroundings and to understand what they are seeing, feeling, hearing, tasting and even smelling. This takes training and, to some extent, maturity.

Anticipation

According to the *Collins English Dictionary*, anticipation is:

'the act of anticipating; expectation, premonition, or foresight'

A performer with a high level of anticipation never looks rushed and seems to be able to predict what is going to happen next and react appropriately. There are many sportsmen and women who display these characteristics and can react early to what is about to happen.

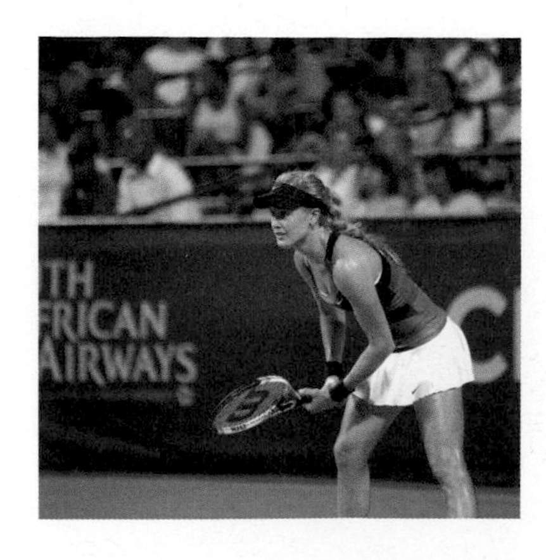

In tennis, a player with good anticipation arrives early to the correct place to retrieve the ball and therefore has time to choose the right option. In fact, a service travelling at 100 mph allows the receiver only half a second to:

- Gauge what type of spin is on the ball
- Predict where the ball will land
- Move to where the ball is going to land
- Decide what type of return to play.

Anticipation is related to what a performer sees needs to be done in a performance context. If the performer is able to anticipate what is going to happen then he has more time to react quickly and see what decision has to be taken.

Anticipation means reaction time will be reduced.

Anticipation is closely linked to the information-processing model. In this model, the performer receives **input** in the form of cues and signals. An example in a hockey game would be a defender watching a player come towards her with the ball. The types of information being received at this stage are shown in the figure to the right.

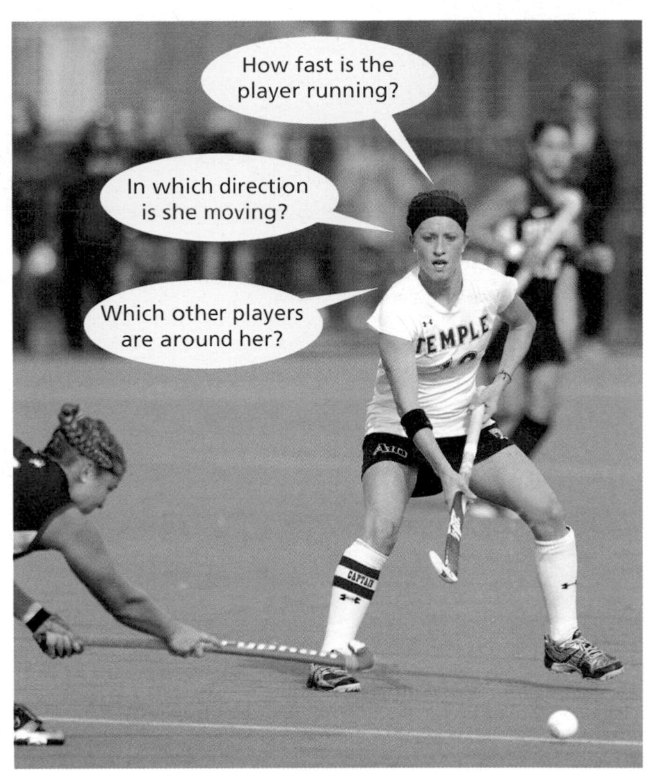

As the brain receives this information, it processes what it sees and in a split second makes decisions about what to do. Anticipation plays a part in what decision is taken. This is because the brain very quickly uses other information **as well** as the input it has received from watching the approaching player – for example the defender's past experience of the player with the ball will influence the decision taken. If the defender remembers that the last time this player came at her she used her reverse stick to go past her, then she is likely to **anticipate** her doing the same thing again.

A very skilled performer will use the cues and signals received at the **input stage** along with previous history of the performance context to make appropriate **decisions**. Coupled with that, the skilled performer will use her instinct to help her make the final decision on what to do. Instinct is almost a guess but it is based on previous history and the success or failure of decisions made in the past. This is the **feedback** part of the information-processing model.

Remember, this all happens in a split second.

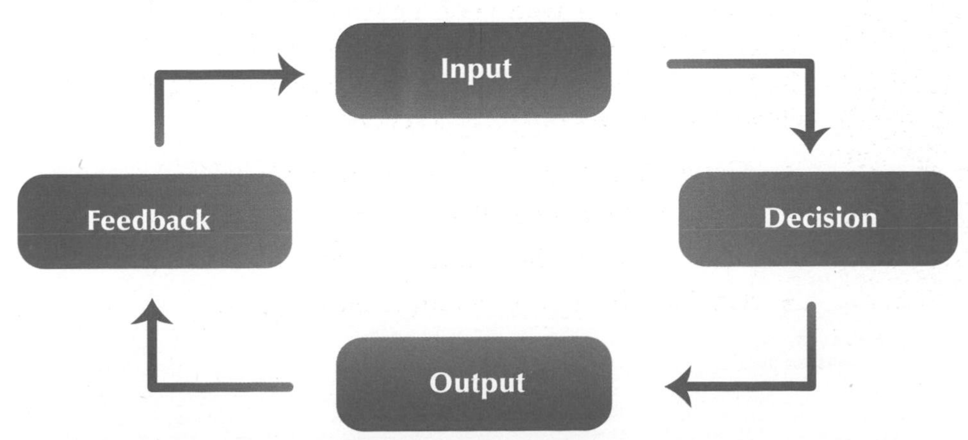

Activity	Anticipation used to:
Badminton 	Work out where the service is going by looking at opponent's stance, racquet and hand position to check for any signals or cues.
Netball 	Work out who the centre pass is going to by reflecting on who received the ball last, who the Centre is looking at, who looks most ready.
Swimming 	Listen and wait to react to the starter's gun going off.
Running 	Work out when to 'go' to overtake another runner by reflecting on what stage it is in the race, whether the leader looks tired, whether he has saved some energy for last minute sprint.
Cricket 	Work out what type of bowl you will receive by observing how the ball is being held, which is the bowler's preferred type of bowl.
Dance 	Work out where partner will land after a jump to be ready to begin a sequence together by watching if she has taken off from the correct place, does she look balanced?

When we understand that anticipation is early decision-making, we can begin to see how it can be used to our advantage when performing. Anticipating something happening means we can scan the performance environment and make decisions to help us separate important information or 'cues' from information we can safely ignore. This all happens in a split second.

By being able to anticipate what is going to happen in a performance situation, we give ourselves extra time to prepare for the decisions we need to take next. In some activities, having this early decision-making ability means the performer looks at ease, arrives early to play the shuttle or ball and generally seems to be in control of their own performance.

Competing against someone with good anticipation is very frustrating. It can feel like an opponent is one step ahead of you and that everything you try to do is ineffective. A person with good anticipation can dictate play and force mistakes to be made. Of course, in a competition, if a performer anticipates wrongly they can look quite foolish. **Successful deception can often be as a result of unsuccessful anticipation.**

Activity 5.3

Watch these clips where the player has obviously wrongly anticipated the return and is completely wrongfooted by the decision the opponent takes.

https://www.youtube.com/watch?v=fxQRmVkGiBU

In creative activities, anticipating what comes next in a sequence or dance is a very positive skill. This would mean that as you were finishing one skill, you were already preparing to begin the next.

Assessment in PE

1.2 Evaluating the impact of positive and negative factors on a performance

By showing you understand the positive and negative impacts of anticipation, you will achieve this assessment standard.

Interesting fact

In the Glasgow 2014 Commonwealth Games there was a 41-stroke table tennis rally between Toriola of Nigeria and Gao of Singapore demonstrating amazing anticipation from both players.

http://www.youtube.com/watch?v=ahOnhEvMgq0

Cues

Anticipation is all about cues. Cues are signals to which we must respond. Therefore, when we are at the early stages of learning, we need help to identify the cues that occur in an activity. At the cognitive stage of learning cue recognition is virtually impossible for the performer as she is probably only concerned with her own execution of skills and has very little ability to watch for what the opponent is going to do. Therefore, anticipation is only really possible for performers with fairly well established skills, near if not in the automatic stage of learning.

The cues that we pick up as we perform can be:

- Technical – what position the arm is in as it hits the ball
- Tactical – something you pick up as the performance continues, e.g. patterns of play, patterns of movements. This is based on your previous knowledge of this opponent, this activity and even personal experience.

Activity 5.4

In an activity from your course, identify the cues that occur within your performance.

Here is an example:

Activity	Cue	What this tells us
Volleyball	The server hits the ball from behind his head.	The service will have a higher trajectory and is probably going to travel deep into our court.

Make the link

In drama, you will have learned about cues. These are the lines or actions someone who is acting alongside you in a play gives to indicate that you should speak or do something. You must concentrate, listen and watch for the cues. The earlier you can anticipate it being said, the more ready you will be to contribute.

It is important to understand that having the ability to anticipate what your own group or team is going to do is just as important as being able to anticipate what another group or team are going to do.

For example, a setter in volleyball must be able to read the first pass on receipt of service. If she is ready to anticipate where that pass is going to go based on her knowledge of her own team's ability, then she will be more than ready to set the ball and have plenty of time to decide who and where to set the ball to.

She will do this by observing the receiver to check:

- how the receiver gets into position for the service
- if she is controlled
- if she is rushed

- if she is balanced
- if the ball strikes her arms evenly
- if she has cushioned the ball.

In fact, in this activity a role has been created for a player who has exceptional anticipation skills. This person is called the 'libero'. Her role is to anticipate quickly the cues from the opposition indicating where the ball is going to go. Also, within her own team, she needs to pick up the ball if it comes off the block. She has to anticipate where to dive to save the ball going out of court or hitting the floor.

In dance groups, performers are taught to watch each other and to use their peripheral vision to stay in time and in step with the others in their group. This includes thinking not just for themselves but for the others in the group. In this way they will anticipate what is coming next, adjust to compensate for other dancers' decisions and work together as a unit.

In gymnastics, anticipation is needed to adjust position after landing in a sequence to ensure you are more than ready to execute the next skill. A gymnast's execution of the sequence would be erratic and wouldn't be smooth in a performance lacking anticipation. As she went from one skill to the next, it may look rushed and she may not appear 'ready' to move to the next skill. Anticipating what is to be done as a sequence is carried out will remind the performer which direction she must be facing in anticipation of completing the **next** skill.

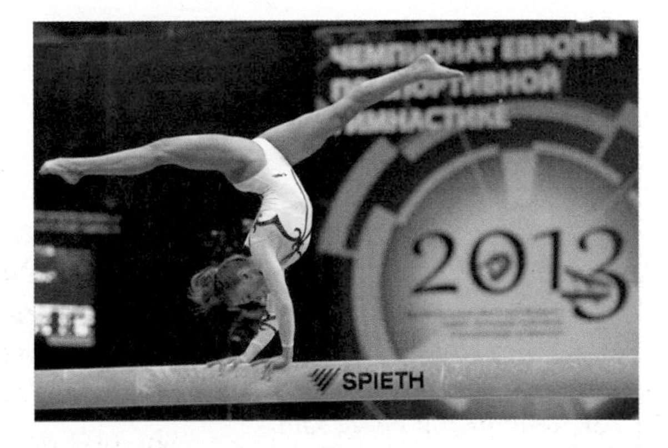

In badminton, a player with poor anticipation would be 'chasing' the shuttle around the court. He would arrive late to the place where the shuttle was played and his response would be rushed and probably ineffective.

Approaches to develop anticipation

To develop anticipation, scientists have recorded versions of performances for athletes to watch back. In this approach, the performer watches clips of the activity. At crucial points, the screen goes blank and the performer must try to explain or predict what happens next.

For example, a clip of a bowler in cricket is shown right up to the moment where the ball is ready to be struck by the hitter. In the training using this approach, the performer who is watching has to identify and explain what type of hit should be used based on all of the evidence he had gathered from the bowler's approach and his arm action.

The theory is that the performer will recognise different cues given by the bowler that then give him clues as to what kind of bowl is about to be used. The clues help the performer decide what is the best reply or shot to play in response. This would mean when in a live performance situation, the performer would be experienced in being able to identify quickly the likely bowl he was going to receive. Consequently he would be prepared early to respond appropriately.

Interesting fact

Many national teams now train the eyes to work quickly to enable them to be able to move in any direction as fast as possible. They train the eyes by using computer programmes which make the head stay still while the eyes are moved from right to left to up and down. This means the eye muscles are in tip-top condition to move to see cues wherever they might happen in the playing environment.

In your course it would be very difficult to obtain the type of technology required to use this approach. However, in order to be able to get exposure to the types of cues you should look for in a performance, it would be very useful to film model performances and to identify the kinds of things that would affect the decisions you have to make. In this way you are learning about the times in an activity when you need to make these early decisions, i.e. to **anticipate**.

There are two approaches that are very useful to develop anticipation. These are:

- The structured approach
- The unstructured approach.

The structured approach

The **structured approach** is learning by breaking down the performance into set pieces and identifying specific solutions that match the demands of specific performance contexts. The structured approach deals with one performance situation at a time. This means it matches problem (a) with solution (a).

Step 1

This would involve identifying key areas within the performance where anticipation would be beneficial. This might take the form of watching a video of your performance to enable you to see times when you were aware or unaware of what the opposition or others in your group were doing. Essentially, you are looking to identify cues to which you really should be ready to react.

Step 2

When a missed cue has been identified, a possible solution can be discussed. For example, watching a playback of a set play in basketball by a previous opposition can enable a defender to identify a signal to set a screen. Or, in netball, recognising when the wing defence leaves her opponent to double block the goal attack, getting out of the centre third to get into her own shooting circle.

Step 3

Having agreed the best solution available, you should plan to actually try the solution in a live performance. By seeing the performance problems, discussing them and then coming up with possible solutions, confidence and success can almost be guaranteed the next time this problem is faced.

Step 4

An evaluation of your choice of solution and its application in the live performance should be undertaken. Specifically, when the performance required you to make an early decision, did you manage to do so, and was your action successful? Or would another solution have been more appropriate? If this was the case you should go back into the 'set piece' of the performance and make use of the alternative solution. Again, an evaluation of the success or otherwise would be necessary.

Step 5

Individuals or members of a group or team should rehearse the problem and correct solution together. In this way you are linking a correct response to a given problem.

In a performance situation, this correct response should automatically be the response to the situation in which you find yourself.

The unstructured approach

Let's move on to the next approach, which is the **unstructured approach**.

A description of this approach would include details of the types of drills used where **more than one** performance problem was presented and where **more than one** solution was possible.

In effect, coached games or unpredictable drills are organised where particular problems occur and require the performer to respond as early as possible with the correct solution.

In this setting, the performer is under less pressure than he would be in the live performance and so there is the facility to stop the game and to highlight **when** cues were missed or misinterpreted.

In preparation for your course assessment for performance, it is likely you will work through a variety of performance scenarios where you will practise scanning for cues that are important and for those that are not. This will help you to develop your anticipation skills.

You will become more skilled at identifying the things someone else does that, in turn, affect your own performance. Throughout these scenarios you will have the opportunity to gain exposure to the variety of situations where anticipation is required.

Your teacher might stop the activity and point out the cues that are available. You will be encouraged to reflect on what you should do, what options are available to you and also to remember what you did the last time you faced this situation. These are all examples of using an unstructured approach to develop anticipation.

As anticipation is affected by prior knowledge about the performance situation, the more times you face a performance problem and arrive at the correct solution, the quicker your anticipation will be the very next time you come up against it.

An example of using this unstructured approach might be, in a tennis game, to have a right-handed player playing against a left hander. The game would be set up and allowed to continue through to completion if it was being recorded. This would allow a retrospective reflection using the unstructured approach. The benefits of this are that you can view the performance at a later time and spend more time analysing what cues were evident, which were missed and which were seen and responded to effectively.

Interesting fact

Tennis player Rafael Nadal is left-handed only when playing tennis – he writes with his right hand. His coach and Uncle Toni Nadal noticed that Nadal was comfortable playing with both hands and encouraged him to play with his left hand as an advantage over the opposition.

Benefits of using this approach

This unstructured approach to developing anticipation has proved very positive in bringing about improved performance in live situations because of its very close links to the actual demands of a real performance.

Limitations to using this approach

There is debate about the validity of delaying the feedback to the performer when developing anticipation. It has been said that stopping the performance immediately after a cue is missed is more beneficial to the performer, as it instantly requires recall from the performer about what happened. Evidence suggests that this instant feedback allows the performer to internalise immediately the missed opportunity for anticipation. This is obviously not possible in a live performance context.

Assessment in PE

2.4 Evaluating the effectiveness of the development plan and the methods used to monitor development

Making use of these approaches and comparing results before and after can prove the effectiveness of the development plan.

Check your progress

	HELP NEEDED	GETTING THERE	CONFIDENT
1. Explain the difference between resilience and mental toughness.			

Advice from marker – Give details about what each feature is and then the reasons why mental toughness is more about preparing for a difficult challenge and resilience is more about recovering from setbacks if they come along.

	HELP NEEDED	GETTING THERE	CONFIDENT
2. Research sports/activities where high levels of mental toughness are required. Explain what the challenges are in these sports/activities.			

Advice from marker – Look at some sports that last a long time, are physically or mentally challenging and where performers have to be mentally tough. Give reasons why the challenges they have to face are particularly difficult.

	HELP NEEDED	GETTING THERE	CONFIDENT
3. Describe how you might use your senses to help you use the success imagery approach.			

Advice from marker – How would you use each sense when using this approach? Explain why the unstructured approach might be more useful in open situations when more than one specific cue might be present and more than one response is possible.

	HELP NEEDED	GETTING THERE	CONFIDENT
4. Explain how anticipation would help you in any activity.			

Advice from marker – Give reasons why you need to react early to a cue, what benefits there are in being first off the blocks, how you might intercept the ball more often with good anticipation. What information would you get from your sight, your hearing, etc.?

	HELP NEEDED	GETTING THERE	CONFIDENT
5. Describe how the structured approach allows you to focus on one specific aspect of performance that requires good anticipation.			

Advice from marker – Describe working on service reception to the back hand alone, for example with the performer rehearsing and practising a top spin reply to this serve in isolation with no other variation in response required.

	HELP NEEDED	GETTING THERE	CONFIDENT
6. Explain why the unstructured approach might be more useful in open situations when more than one specific cue might be present and more than one response is possible.			

Advice from marker – Give details of the variety the unstructured approach allows, how it is more game-like and how the skills developed during practice might be able to be transferred back into the game more readily.

6 Approaches to develop the emotional factor

In this chapter you will learn:

1. How self-control and anxiety can impact positively and negatively on performance.
2. To understand, apply and evaluate approaches to develop self-control and anxiety management.

What should I already know?

The emotional factor is an area that you might have investigated at National 4 or 5. At this level you will have examined how emotions have a positive or negative impact on your performance. At Higher you will look at this factor and investigate how it impacts on your performance across a range of activities. The knowledge and skills you acquire can then be used to develop your understanding of how this can be applied to help you solve performance problems.

Within the emotional factor you will look at the range of emotions that can affect your performance. These emotions are:

- Happiness
- Anger
- Fear
- Trust
- Surprise

These emotions are interesting because they can be interconnected and can affect each other as you perform. For example, if a competitor in a dance competition introduces a new motif that is very difficult and very interesting, then the **surprise** you get might affect your confidence (**happiness**) when you go on to perform your own dance. You might **panic** as you begin to think your dance is not good enough to compete and, as a result, you get **angry** and **frustrated** and make some mistakes.

In this book we will look at two of the features associated with this factor and we will look at a number of approaches to deal with the positive and negative impact of these features on performance.

The features we will examine are:

- Self-control (**anger**)
- Anxiety (**fear**)

Self-control (from the emotion anger)

It could be said that self-control is a necessary requirement in all activities. If you are in control of your emotions, then it is safe to say you will not get angry at yourself or at others around you. This would make self-control a positive influence on your performance. If you are in control of your emotions, you can deal well with the demands of a performance.

Skills for life, learning and work

Self-control is a very important characteristic in work and play. When you are faced with decisions you do not like or do not want to accept, you must learn to exercise self-control. As you mature and get more experienced, self-control becomes a little easier to manage. An employee who can manage their emotions is more reliable and effective than one who loses control in a stressful situation.

Activity 6.1

Look at the following YouTube clip to see the impact lack of self-control can have in a competitive tennis match. http://www.youtube.com/watch?v=C8Nyc9jzSDg

The negative and positive impact of self-control

Self-control can help or hinder you by forcing you to deal with the emotions experienced when you:

- have suffered what you feel is a bad decision from an official
- have to deal with an aggressive opponent
- are on the receiving end of a foul
- have to deal with the disappointment associated with losing
- have to deal with happiness/excitement associated with winning
- make a mistake
- receive criticism about your performance
- are substituted.

Dealing with a bad decision from an official

If an official makes a decision you do not agree with during a performance, it is possible you could lose self-control. This might show itself in the following ways:

- You shout or argue with the official.
- You lose your temper and then give up.

This might result in you:

- being sent off, disciplined or disqualified
- experiencing your own performance deteriorate, which could negatively influence the performances of those around you if you are in a team or group.

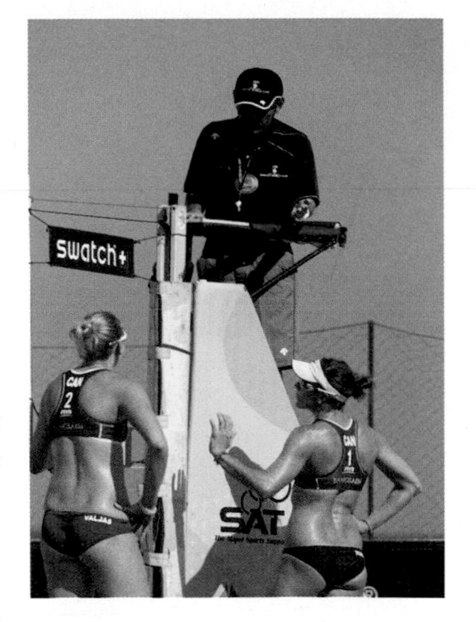

Dealing with an aggressive opponent

When trying to deal with an aggressive player or performer, it is possible you will lose self-control. This might show itself in the following ways:

- You might end up arguing with the opponent or an official.
- You might become aggressive too.
- You might feel frustrated and end up making rash tackles, passes or rush your performance.

This might result in:

- you being disciplined because of your behaviour or attitude
- your performance deteriorating.

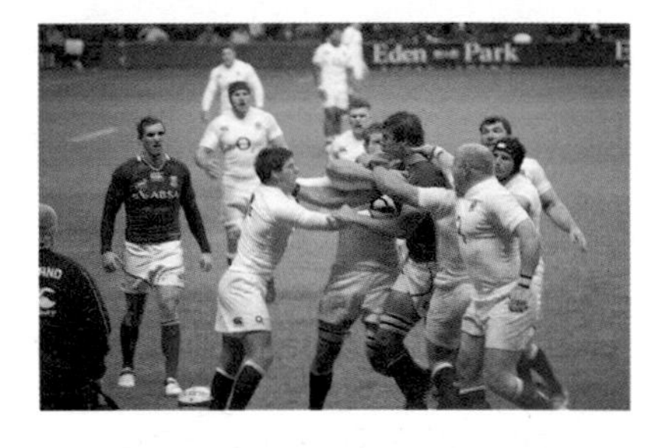

Dealing with a foul on you

While playing a sport, if you are fouled because of something the opposition does, it is possible you will lose self-control. This might show itself in the following ways:

- You might foul the player in retaliation.
- You might argue with the player or officials.

This might result in you:

- being disciplined or sent off
- continuing with a bad attitude and poor concentration.

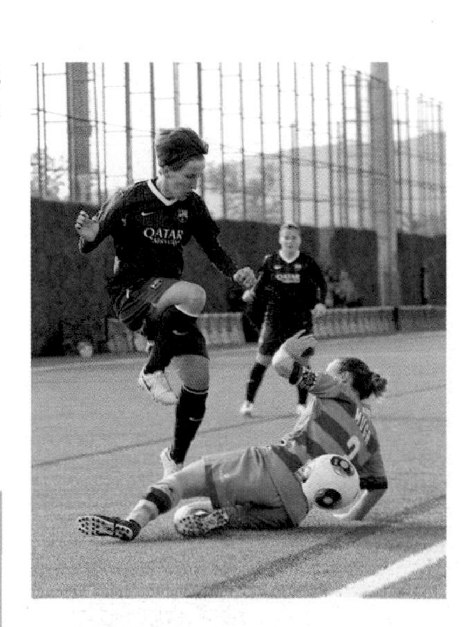

> **Interesting fact**
>
> Brazil, the host nation of the 2014 World Cup, was given the highest number of bookings in the tournament. They received 14 yellow cards overall.

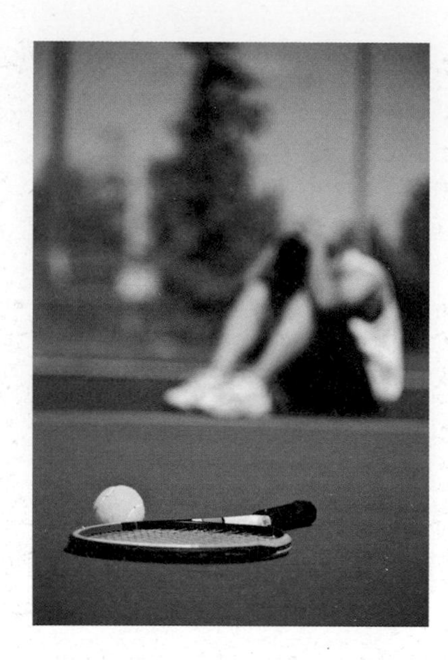

Dealing with disappointment associated with losing

If you begin to feel as though you can't win or indeed have lost at the end of a performance, it is possible you might lose self-control. This might show itself in the following ways:

- You might give up.
- You may say or do something reckless.

This might result in you:

- losing by an even bigger margin
- being disciplined, disqualified or being sent off.

Dealing with emotions associated with winning

If you begin to feel as though you could win during a performance, or if you do in fact win, it is possible you might lose self-control. This might show itself in the following ways:

- You might lose focus and concentration.
- You might take 'your foot off the accelerator' and relax.

This might result in you:

- losing points or control of the performance
- allowing the opposition to 'come back into the game'.

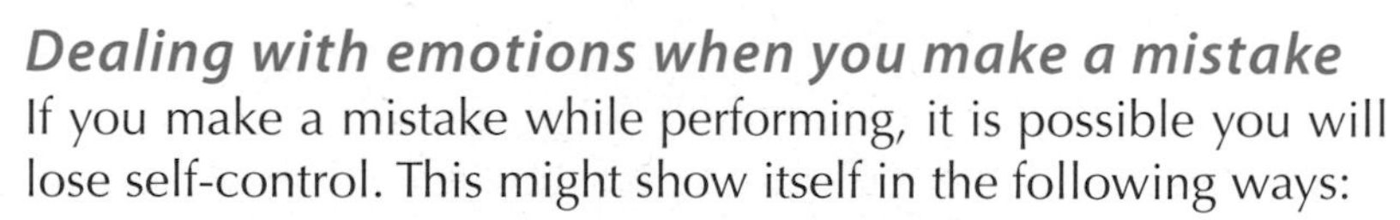

Dealing with emotions when you make a mistake

If you make a mistake while performing, it is possible you will lose self-control. This might show itself in the following ways:

- You might feel frustrated and be tempted to give up or stop trying hard.
- You may lose confidence and stop tackling/passing for fear of making more mistakes.

This might result in you:

- not giving a good, strong performance
- losing or becoming a weak link in your team or group.

Dealing with criticism about your performance

If you receive negative/critical feedback during a performance from a coach, fellow performer/competitor, or even an audience or crowd, it is possible you will lose self-control. This might show itself in the following ways:

- You might 'pull back', become less involved, try less or try to 'hide' in a group performance.
- You might argue or behave in an aggressive way to try to defend yourself.

This might result in you:

- losing focus on the performance
- becoming less involved and motivated to do your best.

Dealing with feelings when substituted

If you are substituted unexpectedly, it is possible you will lose self-control. This might show itself in the following way:

- You might dispute the substitution with your coach or captain.

This might result in you:

- being distracted and disrupting the performance of the oncoming sub and the rest of the team.

Assessment in PE

1.2 Evaluating the impact of positive and negative factors on a performance

Using some of the information discussed in this chapter will help you to evaluate whether these features have an impact on your performance.

Losing self-control can have a very negative impact on your own performance and also on the performances of those around you. In the many situations you find yourself in when performing, effective management of emotions is a basic requirement to enable you to give your best performance. Being able to concentrate on what the body has to do and what decisions have to be made, without the distraction of negative feelings that come about because of issues with self-control, makes success more likely.

Approaches to develop self-control

The following are some approaches that can assist in helping performers to **establish**, **maintain** or **regain** self-control.

Recognising when you are in control of your emotions is a worthwhile skill. You should reflect back to the chapter on collecting data on the emotional factor to help you identify instances when you controlled the impact of emotions on your performance.

Positive outlook approach

Self-control can be **established** by using a **positive outlook approach**. This means you deliberately intend to focus on the positive aspects of your previous performances to help you prepare for the next. Instead of dwelling on mistakes or poor decisions you made in your last performance, you must identify two areas where you did something successfully and made a positive impact on the overall performance. As you reflect on these positive contributions, you should try to identify the feelings you are experiencing. This links the feelings with the positive outcome. It also deliberately blocks the influence of any negative emotions as you attempt to prepare for performance.

I supported the attack as they moved up field and helped set up the winning goal in the first half.

I made sure I marked my opponent tightly and denied her any real attacking opportunities.

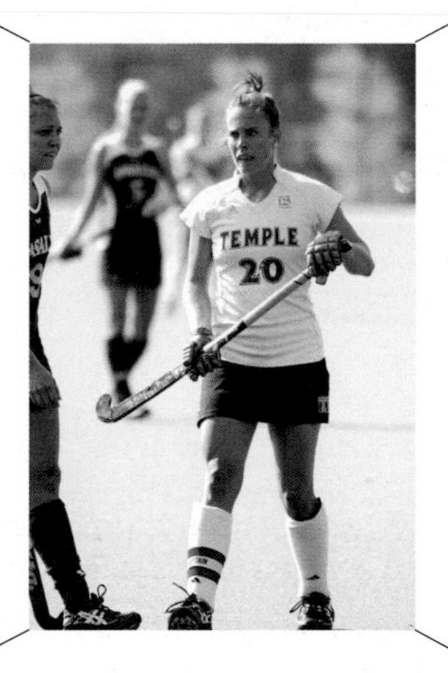

I was able to stay focused and so managed to intercept the ball twice as it was played through the defence.

I successfully delayed the oncoming striker to give my defence time to get back and cover.

Activity 6.2

Carry out this **positive outlook approach** before a performance.

Find a quiet place to sit where you will be uninterrupted.

Step 1: Reflect on the previous performance you gave.

Step 2: Write down two things that you believe you did well.

Step 3: Choose **one** of the aspects identified and 'run over' this in your mind. Ask yourself – what did I do, who was there, what impact did it have on the performance?

Step 4: Try to remember what if **felt** like when you were going through this successful part of your performance. Write down these feelings.

Repeat **Step 3** for another aspect.

This approach encourages the mind to set itself in a positive state. This means a state of self-control is established. This is where the emotions are under control and consequently the mind is able to focus on what is required within the performance.

Benefits of using this approach

This approach allows the performer to have some ownership over the way she feels. It encourages self-reflection and a degree of appreciation of the circumstances in which the performer might find herself. By taking responsibility for identifying those things that went well and that illustrate when she was in control, the theory is that the performer will set aside, and move on from, the mistakes she made before, during and after she lost control. The positive outlook approach requires a determined effort by the performer to avoid being in the negative situation again by focusing on the parts of the performance that were successful in the hope that these would be repeated.

Limitations of using this approach

In the heat of the moment it may not be possible to make use of this approach right away. This might be because the loss **of self-control** has resulted in the player being disciplined or even sent off. When emotions run out of control it is a very difficult process to bring them back under control quickly, especially if there have been many negative things that have added together to make the performer lose control.

Skills for Life learning and work

There will be many circumstances in life where self-control must be established before some sort of action is taken. For example, before an exam the impact of fear of failure might make you lose self-control and burst into tears. This would obviously mean you would not do as well as you had planned to do.

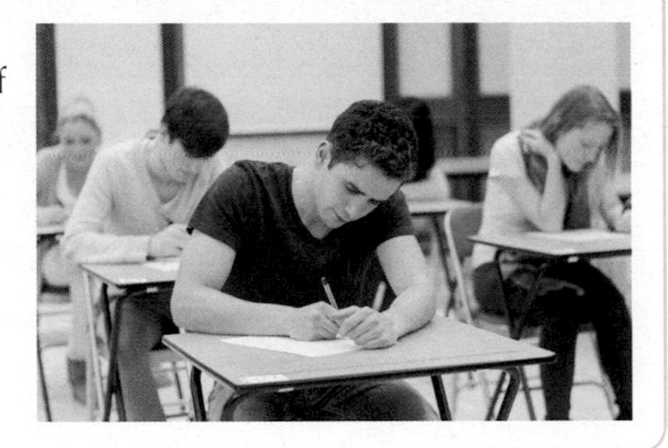

'Parking it' approach

A second approach that can be used to maintain self-control while performing is **'Parking it'**. This approach involves a performer trying to put to one side something that occurs which threatens to make him/her lose self-control – for example, being on the receiving end of a bad tackle, losing points quickly in a game, or making a mistake in the first few seconds of a dance. The theory is that when an incident occurs, you attempt to 'park it' with the intention of going back and 'picking it up' later when you have time to deal with it. This is much like parking your car while you go shopping for some new clothes. You do not think about the car while you are shopping and are able to carry on buying all you intended to buy. Once finished, you return to collect the car from where you left it.

In a performance situation you would acknowledge the mistake or bad tackle, but then make a conscious effort to 'park it' and move on with the performance.

Here is an example:

A netballer who is contacted by her opponent feels angry as she was knocked over onto the floor. As she stands up, she says 'park it' to herself and takes the ball from the umpire to take the penalty pass. This means there is no wasted time shouting at the opponent or appealing to the umpire to take action. Both these responses would impact on her performance. Instead, she is able to take complete control of her play and shut out the distraction and disruption this foul could have caused her.

Make the link

By preparing in this way for performance, the **physical factor** can also be positively impacted, as you are able to focus on the tactics and skills you need to use within your performance.

By preparing like this for a performance, the **mental factor** can also be positively impacted, as you are more likely to make correct decisions when required.

This approach can also impact the **social factor** positively. You are less likely to be a liability to the team or group you are working with since you should be able to carry out your role and contribute to the overall demands of the performance.

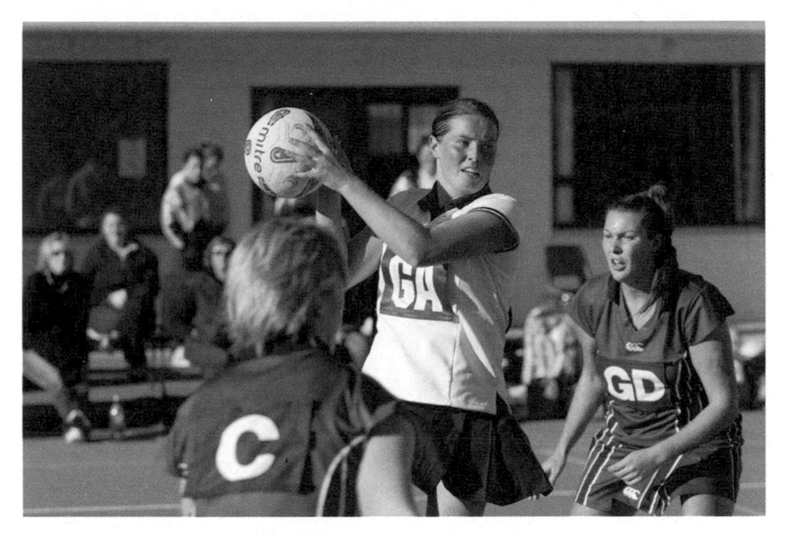

In some sports, attempting to make opposition players lose self-control is encouraged. Some football managers advise their defenders to mark extremely tightly in the first few minutes and tackle harder and more physically with the intention of trying to make a key player lose self-control. These cynical managers know that a player who loses self-control is easier to deal with than one who is able to stay focused and 'on' their game.

Retaining self-control is an important requirement in all activities.

A brilliant gymnast who is temperamental and loses self-control easily on making a bad landing would find it difficult to carry on and effectively complete the floor routine. This would mean overall points would be low. She might still make the mistake when using the 'park it' approach, but her recovery from it would be instant, meaning the only points lost would be those resulting from the bad landing.

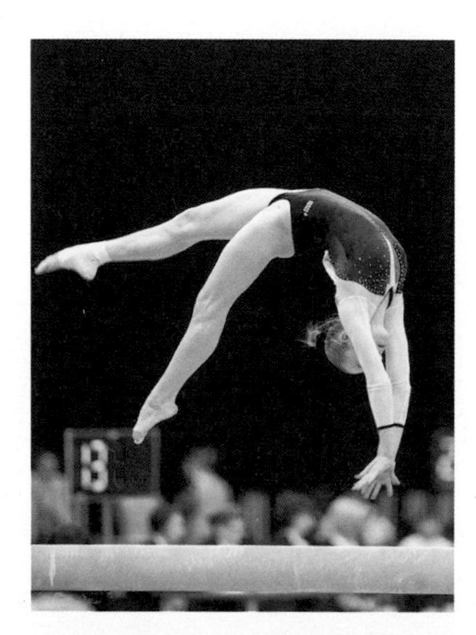

Benefits of using this approach

Much like the 'positive outlook' approach, using this 'park it' approach asks the performer to set aside the failings immediately while performing in order that the remainder of the performance can be completed as effectively as possible. The success of the approach depends on the performer understanding that the focus of attention must change instantly from the mistake to what has to be done next. It is beneficial in a game of tennis if, after losing the tie break, a performer comes out with a new mindset to play the game as if from the very first point. There is no hesitation or fear of defeat, only a renewed spirit to get stuck into the game.

In a netball game, at the end of the first quarter a team might be losing 12–2. Using 'park it' a new strategy is agreed that the team score from every centre pass taken – therefore the previous score becomes unimportant and forgotten about and the team can go back on to play the remaining three quarters feeling invigorated and motivated to do their best.

Limitations of using this approach

Players need to be determined and trained in being able to set aside immediately the incident that allowed them to lose control. This takes time and experience.

Assessment in PE

1.3 Explaining approaches to develop performance based on these evaluations

By being able to **explain** the 'park it' approach you will be able to achieve this assessment standard.

These are areas that will be examined in the final exam.

This '**park it**' approach can be used when self-control is lost and a performer has to try to **regain** focus and continue performing. After an incident where self-control is lost, a performer has to try to put aside the feelings generated and carry on. In this instance it could be a teammate or fellow group member who encourages the performer to 'park it'. Some teams or groups have a signal that teammates can use when there is no opportunity for verbal communication.

Activity 6.3

Can you come up with a signal for 'park it'?

Assessment in PE

1.3 Explaining approaches to develop performance based on these evaluations

Knowledge of these approaches will enable you to achieve this assessment standard.

How would these approaches be incorporated within a development plan?

These approaches (positive outlook and 'parking it') would be part of an overall development programme for performance. Both approaches would be used in training to familiarise the performer with the relevant procedures. This means that, when used in a live performance, the routine or the approach can be the focus for the performer. Time would be set aside at the beginning of any practice performance to allow the performer to make good use of the approach to prepare them emotionally. The approach would be used consistently within every training session or rehearsal to increase familiarity and ease of use. As time progresses, the approach will become part of performance preparation and the only changes that might be made are introducing the examples of good performance recorded as part of the positive outlook approach (see page 106).

Assessment in PE

2.1 Producing a personal development plan that sets appropriate development targets

By planning to focus on improving self-control using these approaches you will be able to achieve this assessment standard.

2.4 Evaluating the effect of the development plan and the methods used to monitor development

By trying to quantify **how much** your performance has improved after carrying out your performance development plan, you will achieve this assessment standard. You should also give judgments about qualitative evidence you have gathered that shows your overall performance could be assessed as having improved. You must also show that you have evaluated how useful your methods of monitoring progress were.

How will you know if the approach is having a positive impact on performance?

You would need to reflect back on the methods used to gather information before you started your performance development plan. You would expect to see that your performance overall was more successful, with fewer instances of you losing control of your emotions. You should feel more in control in situations where things go wrong and see evidence to show this. You should then be able to stay focused on your performance and not be distracted.

Anxiety

You might experience anxiety in different circumstances and the effects on your performance can range from disastrous to minimal. We will look at the impact anxiety can have on your performance and the approaches you can use to manage this emotional response.

Anxiety is defined as:

'A state of uneasiness or tension caused by apprehension of possible future misfortune, danger, etc.; worry.'

Collins English Dictionary

These feelings, experienced by many performers, can be due to our own personality make-up (**trait anxiety**). These traits tend therefore to be more permanent or at least very well established. The other type of anxiety is the reaction a person might have to a stressful environment (**state anxiety**).

There are approaches to deal with both types of anxiety. However, in your course, you will probably focus more on how to deal with the temporary effects of **state anxiety**.

Anxiety can impact upon your performance **psychologically** and **physiologically**.

Psychologically means our thinking or **cognitive** processes are affected.

Physiologically means our body or **somatic** processes are affected.

Assessment in PE

1.2 Evaluating the impact of positive and negative factors on performance

This section should help you to investigate and, to some extent, measure how anxiety impacts on any performance.

Cognitive anxiety

Poor decision-making
Poor attention span
Lack of anticipation
Low level of motivation
Poor listening skills
Poor concentration

We will look first at the possible effects of anxiety on our cognitive processing. The table on the right shows some of the effects anxiety can have on performance.

Anxiety does not have a positive effect on performance, so the management of this emotional factor is important. Every performer must learn approaches to minimise its impact. We will look at these as we go through this section.

Crucially, anxiety affects decision-making in a performance. Poor decision-making within a performance environment can lead to a variety of problems. First, in games, a performer who does the wrong thing, goes to the wrong place, passes instead of shooting, can be responsible for losing the game.

In creative activities, decision-making can also be affected by anxiety. The gymnast might make the decision to 'open out' too early and so fail to complete the somersault perfectly. The dancer might move too quickly towards a partner in a dance and consequently be too early for them to perform the next motif together.

Activity 6.4

Brainstorm all the decisions you need to make when taking part in the games that are part of your course. Write them up in a 'decision outcome' flow chart. Here is an example:

Activity: Volleyball

Possible decision: which set should I use? → Decision taken: reverse set → Outcome: the spiker beat the block

In this situation the setter had more than one option to choose from and so when anxiety is present it is possible that the wrong decision might be taken. Refer back to your flow charts and examine if any of the decisions you took were affected by anxiety.

Sometimes anxiety affects decision-making by forcing the performer to 'freeze'– make no decisions. The impact of this type of decision-making is sometimes easy to see when a goalkeeper has to make a quick decision when trying to save a shot on goal. Their indecision may cause them to come out to save the ball but then hesitate and stop – leaving them in 'no-man's land'.

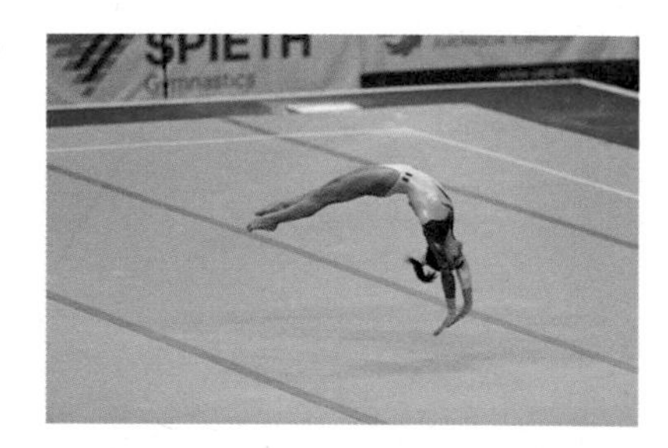

Anxiety can negatively affect what a performer sees (anticipation) or what he chooses to focus on (attention span). This might mean important cues are missed or are seen too late for effective decisions to be made.

Activity 6.5

Many professional sports people have their own ways of preparing for competition. Look at this website, which has many examples of strategies players use to get ready to give their best on the football field.

http://performance.fourfourtwo.com/pro-tips/sebastien-bassong-pre-match-preparation

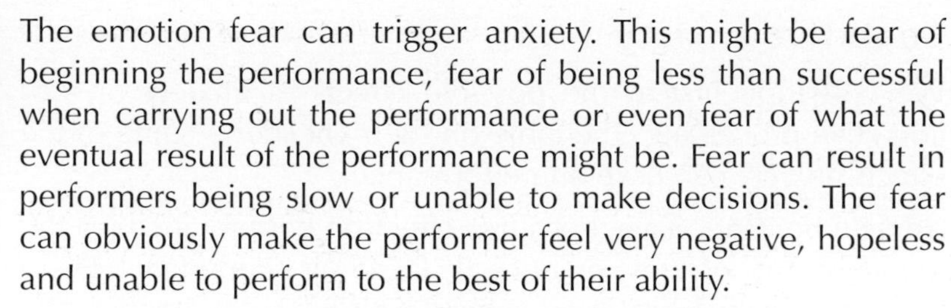

The emotion fear can trigger anxiety. This might be fear of beginning the performance, fear of being less than successful when carrying out the performance or even fear of what the eventual result of the performance might be. Fear can result in performers being slow or unable to make decisions. The fear can obviously make the performer feel very negative, hopeless and unable to perform to the best of their ability.

Low motivation can also come about as anxiety gets a grip on a performer. Low motivation can also impact upon decision-making, as it makes the performer feel uncertain and not care about the quality of their performance.

Anxiety can affect a performer's listening skills. This means that during preparation for performance, instructions might be missed. When the performance is underway, the performer might not fulfil their duties or their sequences/routines effectively.

In the same way, concentration can be impacted by anxiety. Concentration before and during a performance can be impacted or interrupted by anxiety. Again, instructions might be lost or duties not carried out effectively.

Somatic anxiety

Somatic anxiety is the impact of anxiety on the **physiology – the body functions –** of the body. The following table shows some of the effects anxiety can have on performance:

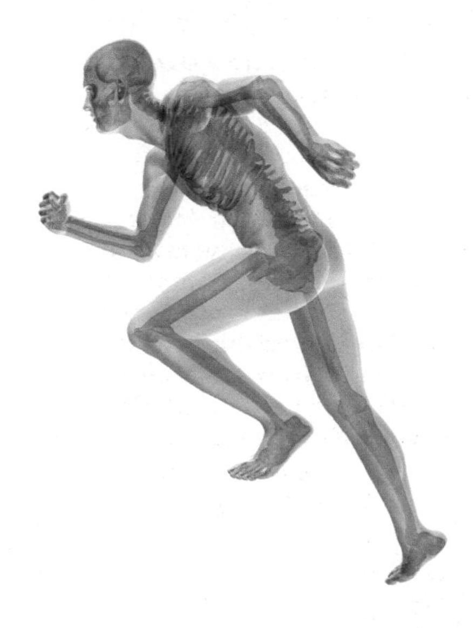

Heart rate increased
Clammy hands
Butterflies in stomach
Feeling sick
Needing the toilet
Babbling
Body shaking

These physical symptoms can affect the way a person performs. They happen as the body tries to deal with the increased feeling of anxiety.

- The increase in heart rate is basically the body trying to work out whether to fight or flight (run away).
- The clammy hands come about as a result of the body sweating because of an increase in body temperature.

- Butterflies in the stomach are the nerves found there being affected by the changes in chemicals the body is producing as a result of anxiety. These can also make you feel sick.
- Needing the toilet is often psychosomatic – something that you **think** you need to do – because you have made a mental note to yourself that you should do it before you perform.
- Babbling, too, is as a result of the increase of chemicals in your blood stream that heighten your awareness and almost make you over alert.

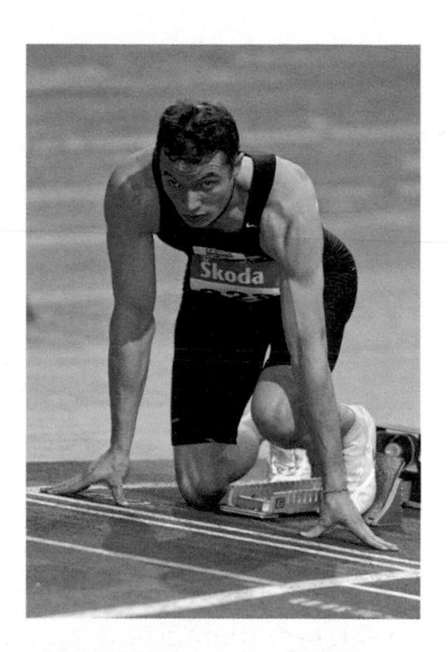

Activity 6.6

Evaluate somatic responses in the activities you do by completing this 'cause and effect' chart. An example has been given for you:

Identify a somatic response you have experienced	Describe how you felt	Evaluate the effect this had on your performance
e.g. I felt sick before I went on to perform	I felt nervous and uncertain about what I was going on to do because this terrible feeling of sickness distracted me. I couldn't remember the first few steps before the music started and I began to feel I might cry and make a fool of myself. I wanted to speak to my teacher to ask her what step I started with and whether I should begin on my right foot. This made me feel even more sick, as my mouth dried up and I had difficulty swallowing.	I didn't take up the correct starting position on the stage, and was too close to one of my group. This made it difficult for her and she got off to a bad start because when we turned we almost collided. I felt the indecision at the beginning made me slow to begin the first few steps. This meant I was slightly out of time with the other dancers and this caused one of the other dancers to lose concentration. She tried to adjust her timing to fit with mine and as a consequence the first 16 counts were messy and out of sync.

Approaches to deal with anxiety

Now that we know the impact of the emotional factor on performance, we can begin to identify approaches that can be used to manage and, most importantly, minimise its negative influence on performance. We will look specifically at two approaches:

- Centering
- Progressive muscular relaxation (PMR).

Centering

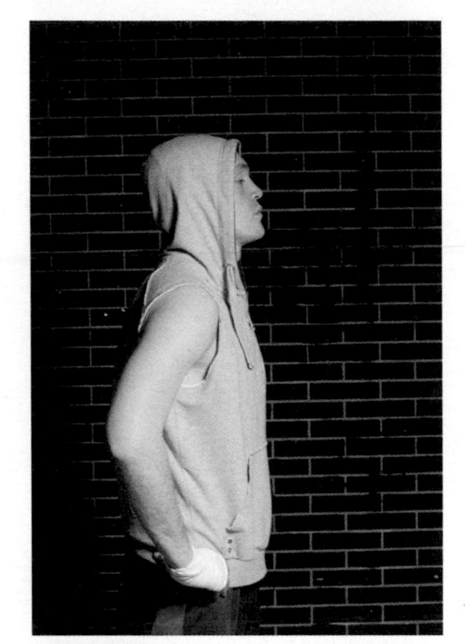

Centering is an approach used by many athletes to manage the effects of anxiety. It is usually used before a performance takes place and is often included in a pre-performance routine. It has seven clearly identified stages with the intention of taking the performer slowly through planned steps to completely replace feelings of anxiety with feelings of control and complete body management.

Here is a description of the centering approach.

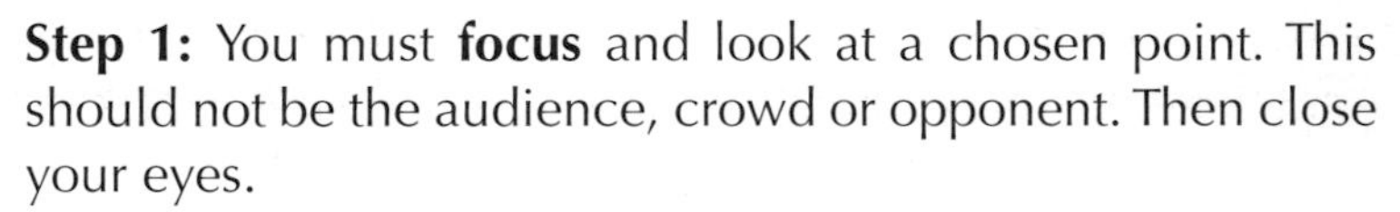

Step 1: You must **focus** and look at a chosen point. This should not be the audience, crowd or opponent. Then close your eyes.

Step 2: With eyes closed, visualise a positive outcome. Look clearly in the 'mind's eye' and replay what a good performance would look like. Run over a few 'clips' of what that successful pass, motif, jump or throw would actually look like.

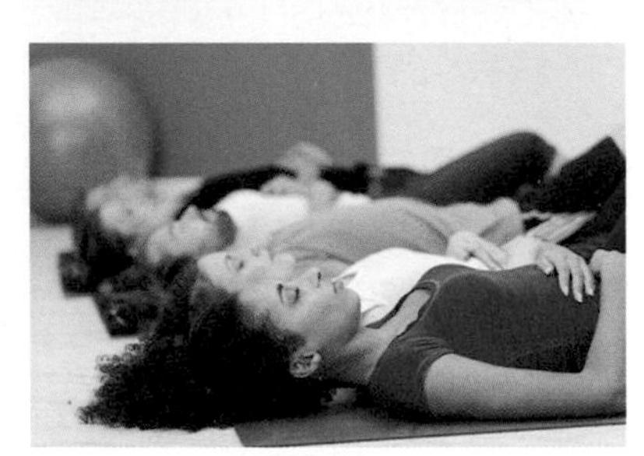

Step 3: Breathe deliberately. That means thinking about what it feels like bringing the air in through the nose and trying to picture this air flooding into the lungs.

Step 4: As this air is contained in the lungs, you must now focus on your centre of gravity, shutting out all distractions. This is **centering**.

Step 5: Consciously release tension from all parts of your body.

Step 6: Prevent any analysis of previous performances by focusing on this centering.

Step 7: Commit to being assertive and commanding right from the beginning of the performance.

Assessment in PE

1.3 Explaining approaches to develop performance based on these evaluations

By explaining – giving the main points and the reasons why this approach is useful for you when focusing on the emotional factor – you will achieve this assessment standard.

Benefits of using this approach

Centering is a useful approach because it is easy to work through step by step.

There is no equipment required and you do the process when it suits you.

You can fit it into pre-performance preparations at a time and place convenient and comfortable for you.

This means you can do it in private and really focus on shutting out anxiety in progressive stages as you personally prepare.

Each of the steps is intended to make you focus less on the somatic responses (bodily reactions to stress) that occur as a result of anxiety.

You make yourself concentrate on positive outcomes and being completely in control of all parts of your body – including your mind.

This encourages the release of tension and promotes the assertiveness you will need to go on and perform positively from the first seconds of your performance.

Ultimately it gives the performer the best chance of achieving success through minimising the impact of anxiety on performance.

Limitations of using this approach

Some performers may feel uneasy carrying out this type of process. It demands a high level of personal responsibility to set aside time to work on their own to deal with the effects of anxiety.

Progressive muscular relaxation

Progressive muscular relaxation (PMR) is a second approach to manage anxiety. It works along the same lines as centering except it requires the performer to progressively take control of all muscle groups within the body. The approach is organised by progressively relaxing and tensing small groups of muscles for 15 seconds at a time.

Here is a description of the approach:

- Find a quiet place to sit or lie depending on your performance environment.
- Start at the face. Tighten the forehead muscle over a period of 15 seconds. Then relax over the same period of 15 seconds.

- Move to the cheeks and repeat.
- Carry on through all muscle groups until you reach the toes.
- As you tighten and relax try to become aware of what muscle tension feels like.

Benefits of using this approach

This approach is worthwhile because it can be done when it suits the performer. It is easy to manage by yourself and can allow you to take personal control over the way you feel and the emotions you are trying to manage. It increases your awareness of muscle groups that are tense and then systematically (in a sensible order) works through relaxing them. This means that the mind and the body's muscles are not experiencing anxiety. Instead the focus can be returned to feeling prepared, relaxed and hopeful about the performance you are about to give. The somatic anxiety is brought into line and the cognitive anxiety is reduced and you are ready to perform.

Limitations of using this approach

Implementing progressive muscular relaxation within a plan of work would involve planning to use this approach every time a performance is required. Time would be essential when preparing for the event, game or competition. It requires good organisation from the performer to set aside enough time in order that the chosen approach is not rushed and does not increase anxiety. Before the beginning of the performance, a performer must be aware how much time is needed to carry out the agreed pre-performance preparation. This means that the approach can be implemented properly in order to impact performance positively.

Assessment in PE

2.1 Producing a personal development plan that sets appropriate development targets

By demonstrating effective planning by including targets for the inclusion of these approaches in a performance development plan, you will achieve this assessment standard.

2.3 Implementing the development plan

By using these approaches in the warm-up routines before you perform, you will demonstrate that you can carry out – or implement – appropriate approaches within a plan to deal with factors that can impact your performance. This means you will satisfy the assessment standard 2.3 above.

Interesting fact

Audley Harrison, super heavyweight boxer and a Commonwealth and Olympic gold medal winner, used Japanese classical music to calm his anxiety before he went on to fight.

Looking back at the performance given before using the approaches would indicate whether they had influenced performance positively. This would require you to evaluate the changes you can see in your whole performance. For example:

- Did you feel less sick?
- Did you feel more positive?
- Did you feel more motivated?
- Was your listening more effective?
- Was your concentration improved?
- Did you feel less frightened?

Regardless of whether the answer to these questions is yes or no, a full and detailed evaluation must include how these affected your overall performance.

Therefore you must include details, such as:

- You used your breathing techniques as part of the centering approach to slow down the production of chemicals that might make you feel sick, resulting in you feeling less sick and therefore able to concentrate better on the position of the hands in the handspring within a sequence.
- Feeling more positive because of the PMR approach allowed you to start the performance relaxed, focused and feeling in control. This meant you weren't put off when you lost four points in quick succession and kept on trying to regain service.
- Having used the centering step 7, where you committed to being assertive right from the beginning, meant you felt more confident to take a chance in using your backhand top spin drive to finish the rally.
- Having used PMR to relax all the muscles meant you listened more effectively and were therefore able to take in more details about the strengths of the opposition goal shooter. You then kept her at the top of the circle in netball to force her to take the distance shot instead of close shots at the post.
- By concentrating better on what you were going to do instead of what you had done in past poor performances at step 6 of centering approach, you were able to anticipate better what foot the striker preferred to take the ball on and so were able to put pressure on him to move the ball to his weaker foot.
- Releasing all tension from your body made you feel less frightened and so able to stick to your game plan when the opposition tried to put you under pressure to play the rallies at their pace.

Assessment in PE

2.4 Evaluating the effectiveness of the development plan and the methods used to monitor development

Detailing the improvements in your performance and relating these to the method you used, as has been done on the previous page, will ensure you achieve this assessment standard.

2.5 Identifying and justifying decisions relating to future personal development needs

It would be safe to say that anxiety can always be a consideration for most performers. Therefore in terms of future needs, the use of these approaches would probably continue throughout a performer's career. This would ensure the negative impact of emotions would be limited. By incorporating these approaches within an overall performance development plan, and showing an appreciation of minimising their impact, you would achieve the assessment standard above.

Check your progress

	HELP NEEDED	GETTING THERE	CONFIDENT
1. Research instances of when performers have lost self-control. Explain what triggered the loss of self-control and evaluate the impact the loss of self-control had on the overall result of the performance. Look first at the Saurez incident clip: https://www.youtube.com/watch?v=O2QAVNjVRPo	○	○	○

Advice from marker – Your explanation must include details of **how** behaviour changed as a result of something that happened and how many points were lost, or by how much the performance deteriorated.

	HELP NEEDED	GETTING THERE	CONFIDENT
2. Describe a situation within or outwith sport when you have lost self-control.	○	○	○

Advice from marker – Your description must give clear details of what the situation was, who was there, who the competition was, was an audience present, etc.

	HELP NEEDED	GETTING THERE	CONFIDENT
3. Identify two approaches to improve self-control. Outline which approach you would prefer to use and then justify your choice.	○	○	○

Advice from marker – You should name the two approaches you know about and then choose one justifying why you prefer this method over the other.

	HELP NEEDED	*GETTING THERE*	*CONFIDENT*
4. Explain the differences between centering and PMR.			

Advice from marker – Give details about what is different about where and when these approaches can be used.

5. Describe the symptoms of somatic anxiety.			

Advice from marker – Give details about what feelings you might experience as a result of this anxiety.

6. Evaluate the impact of cognitive anxiety by comparing your own SCAT test result and that of another performer in your class, team or group.			

Advice from marker – What was your score, how did it compare to others, was it higher or lower, were there similar areas where you scored higher or lower than them?

7 Approaches to develop the social factor

In this chapter you will learn:

1. How working in isolation, communication and gender can impact positively and negatively on performance.
2. To understand, apply and evaluate approaches to deal with working in isolation as well as communication and gender issues.

Within this factor area you will explore how working with others and communicating with others impacts on your performance and how, in some instances, your gender can influence the experience you have when participating in sport or physical activity.

All of these features can influence and impact to a greater or lesser degree a person's performance. We will look closely at three of them and consider approaches that can be used to impact positively on performance.

The three features this book will deal with are:

- Working in isolation
- Gender and peer group issues
- Communication.

What should I already know?

The social factor is an area that you might have investigated at National 4 or 5. At this level you will have examined how different social features might have had a positive or negative impact on your performance. You will be able to use approaches to develop your performance when working on your own or as part of a mixed group where gender may impact group dynamics. In this chapter the feature of communication is included to demonstrate how it can sit within both the physical factor and the social factor. The suggested approaches will enable you to investigate and develop knowledge and skills that will help you work effectively on your own or within a group or team.

Working in isolation

The approaches that will be considered in this section will encourage you to reflect on the performance issues that arise when a performer has to play, perform and perhaps even train on their own.

Working in isolation might also be required within team or group activities. Each person in a team will work to their own individual targets, sometimes in isolation, so there might only be a few times when they come together with members of the group.

This can cause performers to feel isolated and often affects motivation levels. However, it is also possible that some performers enjoy working on their own.

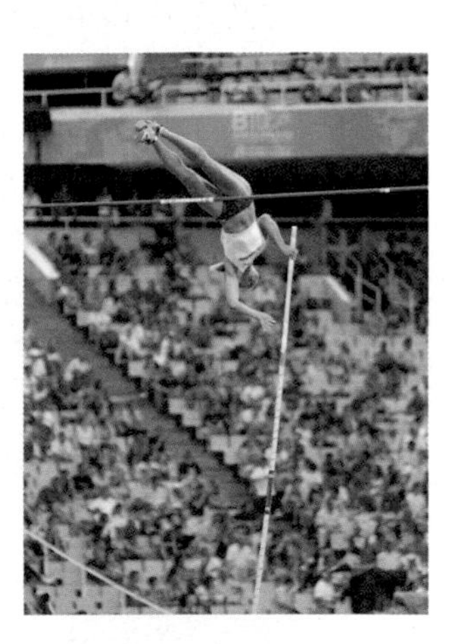

Skills for life, learning and work

Sometimes it is necessary to work on your own. This demands self-discipline and focus to remain on task and to complete it to a high standard.

Working in isolation when preparing for performance

Activity 7.1

Complete this status chart for the activities in which you participate.

Activity	Team or individual activity	Training done as a group or individual

For activities that are performed on your own, training can be completed either on your own or with other performers.

For example:

Activity	Training
Badminton 	Players often work in partnership with other members of a team and share the same coaches and training sessions.
Athletics 	Athletes often work on their own at times of the day that suit them best.
Swimming 	Swimmers almost always take part in team training sessions in the water, but gym and weight training sessions can be completed individually.
Dance 	Most dancers participate in group lessons but would also complete individual focused technique classes, depending on which type of choreography they specialise in.
Netball, football, basketball, rugby, volleyball 	Most members of a team will work together in team training for skills and tactics but will do individualised programmes of work suited to their own fitness levels.

If you are involved in a group outwith your PE class, then it is possible that you will follow the same format as listed on the previous page. It could be also that the activities you are doing within your PE classes are the only time you take part in physical activity or sport.

You need to set up your training to suit your personality and experience, and also your level of determination and motivation. It could be that working on your own while training is not your preferred method. This could be because:

- You are inexperienced at carrying out training programmes.
- You lack motivation when carrying out training programmes.

If you are inexperienced at carrying out training, it is possible that you are unclear about what you have to do, e.g. how many repetitions you should complete or how intensely you should run or swim. It is possible too that the elements included in your programme of work are quite complicated; if you are working on your own you have no one from whom you can seek clarification.

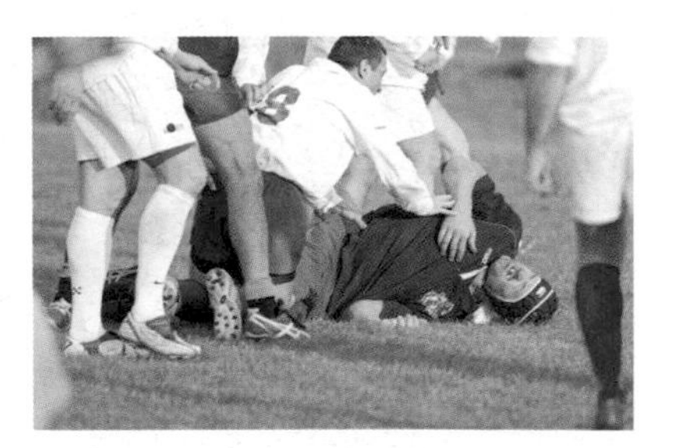

Inexperience in carrying out training could result in a performer getting injured. The supervision provided by an experienced coach is invaluable and means that an inexperienced performer can rely on advice and support relating to:

- exactly what has to be done
- when it is time to change or progress training.

In your course, there might be some parts of your training that are carried out as part of a lesson. However, at Higher level, you are expected to have some knowledge of training approaches.

You might be set tasks to complete certain training sessions outwith class time. This will enable you to make the best possible progress with your training.

Approaches to deal with working in isolation

The referencing approach

If you were an inexperienced performer you would need to take responsibility for your training and use the **referencing approach** while you work.

This means you complete the work you agreed you would do in the allocated session. Once you do this, you should refer back to your coach and check that your intentions for the next session are safe and appropriate. This demands that you keep a detailed training diary so that you can provide evidence of the work you have completed. By following this approach, you can be more assured that the training you are carrying out is actually doing you good.

As you become more confident and gain more knowledge and experience, you will take responsibility for your own performance development. The number of times you need to reference your coach or teacher will decrease. You will need to show that you have produced an appropriate programme of work to impact positively on your performance and be observed carrying it out effectively.

Benefits of using this approach

You will learn to become aware of the changes you see in your performance as you take on more and more responsibility for developing it. Your confidence will grow and as you check out with your teacher or coach and have your intentions confirmed as appropriate, you will become a more successful performer. This means you are less reliant on other people to develop your own personal performance.

Limitations of using this approach

This approach means you have to think and plan for yourself. Some performers are not confident or even willing to think for themselves and so progress might be slow in terms of performance development.

Assessment in PE

1.3 Explain approaches to performance development

2.1 Produce personal development plan

2.3 Implement a development plan

By planning ahead and using this approach to develop your performance while working on your own, you will be able to achieve these assessment standards.

The 'buddy' approach

Another approach you might consider when working in isolation is making use of a training buddy – the **'buddy' approach**.

There are certain benefits and limitations of this approach.

Benefit		Limitation
By making a plan to train alongside someone else you are more likely not to miss training sessions.	**Accountability**	You can sometimes train when over-tired. This might result in overtraining.
A training buddy can give feedback about how a training session went.	**Feedback**	The buddy must be knowledgeable and able to give accurate and meaningful feedback.
An element of competitiveness can increase motivation to constantly increase fitness levels.	**Competition**	Competition can push performers too much and injury can occur.
In some types of training it's necessary to have someone 'spot' you as you lift weights. In others, you might share the interval training rest periods with a partner.	**Support**	Again, your supporter must be reliable and able to carry out the role effectively.
Shared success can be more meaningful and spur on further achievements.	**Achievement**	The intrinsic reward of doing physical activity for its own sake can be lost if constant performance development is the only focus for the performer.

Assessment in PE

1.3 Explaining approaches to develop performance based on these evaluations

By explaining the use of a 'buddy' when training in terms of the accountability, feedback, competition, support and sense of achievement it gives, you will achieve this assessment standard.

You need to ask yourself how self-motivated you are – are competition and a sense of achievement things that would make the **buddy approach** work for your personal needs?

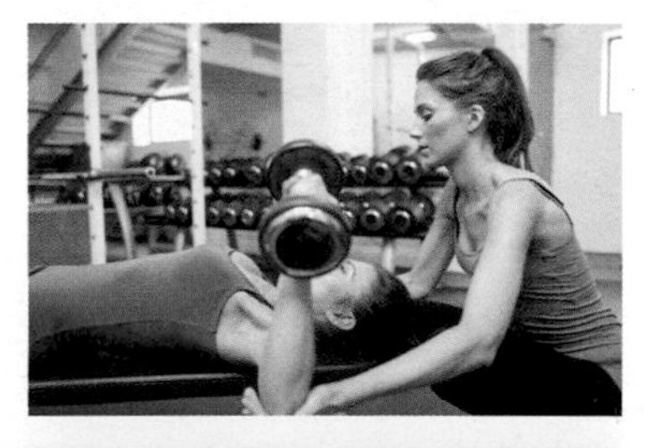

If you find it difficult to work on your own when carrying out a training routine, then teaming up with a buddy can have a positive impact on a training programme and consequently on performance.

If you are required to be the buddy for another performer, then it is important you are aware of the benefits and limitations of this approach.

Whether you prefer to work on your own or with a buddy, you must build activities that suit these preferences into your personal development plan.

Benefits of using this approach

You will find that when working with a 'buddy' who is knowledgeable and supportive that your training will be positive and progressive.

Limitations of using this approach

A 'buddy' who is concerned more with his own performance than yours might not give accurate or helpful feedback. Training would need to be given to the buddy in order that he was able to give accurate feedback. This would take time out of training or preparation for competing.

Working in isolation when performing

Participating in an individual activity can be positive and negative. Sometimes an individual performance can affect a team score, even if it is completed in isolation.

Activity 7.2

Watch the clip of the long jumper. Identify the areas of her performance over which she has had to take complete control. http://www.youtube.com/watch?v=d7gTlJhEwrM

Activity		
100 m sprinter	Individual activity where result affects only the individual performer.	
Beam gymnast	Individual activity where points are awarded to contribute to a team score.	
Golf – Ryder Cup	Scores are collected for each game played and added together towards an overall team score.	
Tennis – Davis Cup	Scores from individual players are added up to give an overall team winner.	

This puts different pressures on a performer. As well as the stress you may feel about your personal performance, there is the added pressure of letting others down who were depending on you to contribute to the overall team success.

The self-focused approach

In this environment, the performer has to use a **self-focused** approach. They must be determined to stick to the successful game plan or strategy they would normally use. The focus during the performance must remain on completing the required skills without the undue distraction of 'doing it for the team'. A performer might lose focus and feel under pressure of letting others down if 'doing it for the team'.

The **self-focused** approach demands that the immediate performance is the focus and that any outside rewards or achievements are set aside for the entire performance. In this way the performer can give his/her complete, undivided attention to what needs to be done. This increases the chance of success and limits the number of mistakes made or poor decisions taken.

In individual activities where the performer is only concerned with her own performance, there are also pressures that can impact negatively:

- Performer can feel isolated
- Performer can feel responsible solely for the outcome of a performance
- Camaraderie is not experienced
- Cooperation is not experienced
- Self-discipline is required at all times
- There is little sense of belonging to a team or group
- Results are not shared or celebrated with fellow performers
- Communication is not a major consideration.

These pressures can lead to dissatisfaction and further isolation.

Sharing common goals, successes and failures enables positive relationships to be built up. These relationships stimulate resilience and positivity, meaning that even when experiencing failure, a performer has a support network available to her through relationships in a team or group. This network gives the performer exposure to camaraderie – a very positive impact of working with others. Camaraderie brings positivity and compassion for members of a group. This stimulates group identity and helps formulate and communicate a shared vision. This leads to cooperation and eliminates the feelings of isolation.

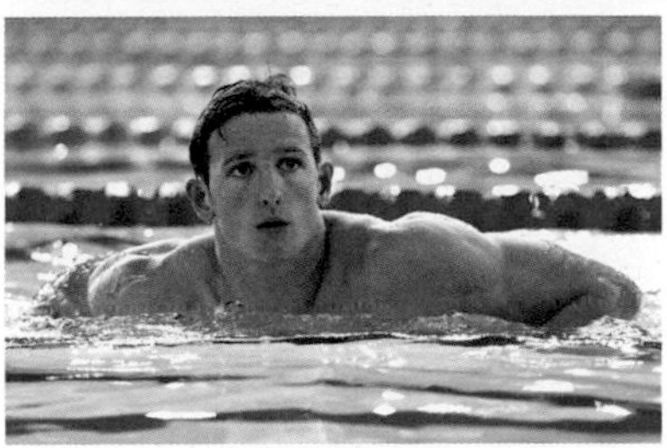

The support approach

Therefore, it is wise to acknowledge that within individual activities a **support approach** should be built in when developing performance. This will ensure the performer has a network of people around them to share the burden of performing.

This would mean the result of a performance could be objectively examined and positives from the performance identified and shared.

It also incorporates accurate positive feedback following the performance. Internal feedback, along with corrective feedback, is a powerful performance development tool.

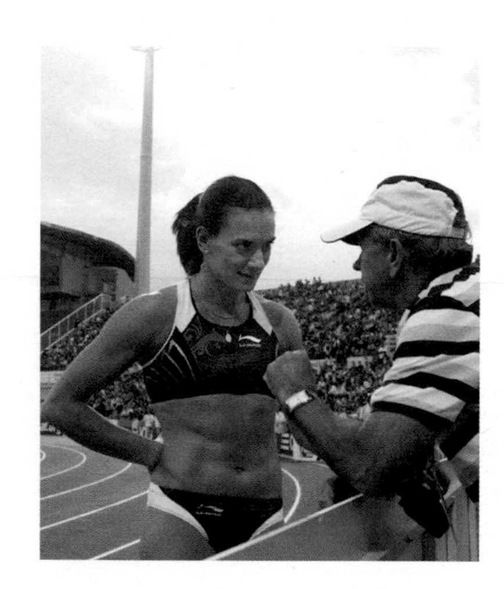

An individual performer does not need a team around them, however; a skilled coach or observer can fulfil many of the duties of a team using this **support approach** and allow the individual competitor to reap the benefits of:

- working with someone towards a common goal
- a sense of camaraderie
- shared success and disappointments
- communicating feelings, fear and concerns.

Benefits of using this approach

Being isolated when performing requires a degree of self-sufficiency. This means you might need to get used to training on your own, motivating yourself to get ready for the next competition or event. This can be tiresome and a real challenge. If a 'support approach' is used then there is more than the performer concerned with the preparation and outcome of the performance. This can create a positive ethos and energise a performer to keep going. He will feel as though it matters to someone other than just himself if there is a 'supporter' who can give some feedback, encourage and generally show an interest in future performances. In some situations parents take on this role.

Limitations of using this approach

As with the buddy approach, training would need to be given to ensure feedback was accurate, meaningful and useful. Parents when taking on this role would need to be careful not to be too critical.

Gender

Gender issues can have a significant impact on your performance, especially if you are a girl who is trying to reach your potential in a male orientated sport. Statistically, females are less likely to take part in sport than males. There are a variety of reasons for this, one being that there are fewer opportunities for females to develop their performance. This can have an impact on their self-esteem and confidence.

This is a good stage to consider the links between the social factor and emotional factor and how, together, they can impact on performance. Females are often identified as thinking more about their feelings and emotions than males. Males, on the other hand, are generally less concerned about these areas. This can impact on performance. For example, a girl might think more about how she feels left out of a game, whereas a boy might decide not to pass the ball to her because she appears disinterested in the game. Communication, a feature that impacts upon both the physical and social factors, could help improve the performance of the team in this situation.

The approaches that are used to improve aspects of performance must suit the needs of both male and female performers' preferences and lifestyles. For example, there are differences between male and female:

- average VO2 max capacity
- strength
- body fat percentages
- range of flexibility.

It is therefore necessary to consider these differences when trying to determine the best approach to use when developing performance.

Interesting fact

In the Olympics there are two sports where women and men compete directly – equestrian disciplines and sailing.

GO! Activity 7.3

In a group, discuss any gender issues that have had an impact on performance. In the table below, list what the issue has been and the impact it may have had on performance.

Gender issue	Impact on performance
E.g. not as fast as the boys in my team	
E.g. girls give up too easily when we are losing	

Approaches to deal with gender issues

Conditioned games approach

In any game, if a player feels left out or not included, the overall performance will be affected. Games should therefore be set up to ensure everyone is involved as much as possible. In training the following would be set up:

- Step 1: Agreed rules of the game would be discussed and agreed. This would include the reasons **why** it was necessary to put these special rules in place. That is, to make use of all players within the team and to encourage all players to try to contribute.
- Step 2: The training session would be carried out and coach feedback given throughout the session in order to reinforce and encourage the group to work together cooperatively.
- Step 3: Coach feedback and individual opportunities to comment on the effectiveness of the conditioned game would be given to all participants. This needs to be managed by an experienced coach or teacher in order that the feedback session remains positive and useful.

Benefits of using this approach

All players within a conditioned game have the opportunity to contribute because the conditions have been set to ensure everyone's involvement. Therefore, everyone's contributions will be acknowledged and individuals can feel valued within the group. Although instances of men and women competing together is limited in amateur and professional sport, in your course it is likely that you may work alongside boys and girls in order to achieve the highest mark possible for your activity. Therefore, in training and when planning to compete against other mixed gender teams, it is essential that everyone plays their part and feels confident that their contributions are appreciated.

Limitations of using this approach

Forced passing to another member of the team who might not be as strong or confident as others within the group can build resentment and confusion. For example, in a conditioned basketball game when at least one pass must go to a girl before a shot is taken, the flow of attack might be negatively affected. The shooter might delay or not take a good shooting opportunity because a pass has still to be made to one female teammate before the shot is taken. This makes the conditions of the game unlike the real live performance situation. It would therefore be fair to question whether or not it was an appropriate game plan to practice.

Also, group dynamics can be adversely affected by the imposition of conditions such as those discussed on the previous page. When the conditions insist a pass has to be made to a female player, it is possible players will be unhappy about 'having' to pass to a player who seems not to be trying as hard, or in as good a position as someone else. This can make relationships strained and have the opposite effects to those intended.

Skills for life, learning and work

There will always be situations in life where you are the more experienced or less experienced employee. Remembering the feelings you experienced when in a performance situation may help you deal more sympathetically with a less experienced or confident co-worker. Patience is required and communication needs to be encouraging and positive. Relationships will then be positive, productive and healthy.

Assessment in PE

1.3 Explaining approaches to develop performance based on these evaluations.

By explaining how you used conditioned games in order to include and involve all players within a game, you will achieve this assessment standard.

How would this approach be incorporated within a development plan?

When preparing for performance, conditioned games would only be used early on in the training session. This is because they are unrealistic conditions and so would need to be removed before focused training began. Therefore, in the first few sessions, conditioned games would take place with the target being to prepare players to work in their real roles with the special conditions removed.

Assessment in PE

2.1 Producing a personal development plan that sets appropriate development targets.

By making use of the conditioned games approach as part of an overall development plan, involvement in a game can be positively influenced.

How will you know if the approach is having a positive impact on performance?

You would need to revisit the data you collected that highlighted the issues relating to gender. The expectation would be for each individual to state they felt more involved in the game after the training with the approach. This would also be shown in an increase in the number of attempts at shooting, possessions and passes to and from each of the players.

Communication

Communication is your ability to share clear and concise information with others who are involved in the activity with you. This may be your teammates, opponents and officials, etc.

Communication involves both listening and speaking.

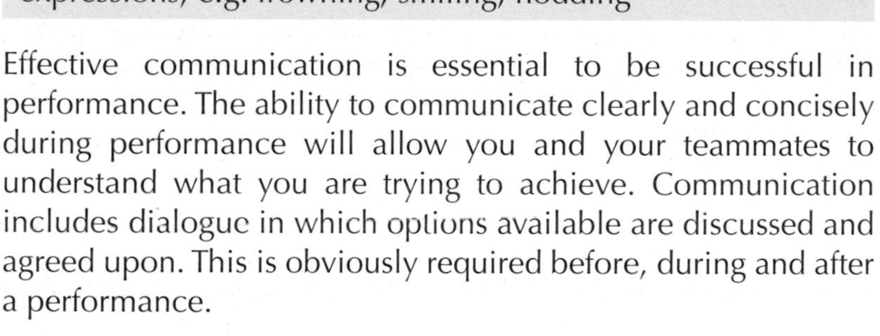

Types of Communication

Verbal Communication: 6 Cs – Clear, Concise, Correct, Complete, Courteous, Constructive

Non verbal Communication: Body Language and facial expressions, e.g. frowning, smiling, nodding

Effective communication is essential to be successful in performance. The ability to communicate clearly and concisely during performance will allow you and your teammates to understand what you are trying to achieve. Communication includes dialogue in which options available are discussed and agreed upon. This is obviously required before, during and after a performance.

Approaches to develop communication

Team communication drills

Drill 1 – Small scale passing drill in a circle. Set a circle of players. Devise different passing options within the circle. The main emphasis will be on communication skills.

- Call out the player's name before making pass.
- Call the name of the person making the pass.
- Use a non verbal signal to receive a pass.

Drill 2 – Passing gauntlet. Two lines of approximately 4 players. Player runs down the line passing and receiving the ball. The main emphasis will be on communication skills.

- Call out the player's name before making pass.
- Call the name of the person making the pass.
- Use a non verbal signal to receive a pass.

Drill 3 – Set up a practice to develop a strategy within your performance. Highlight the types of communication you have to use during this practice.

Conditioned games for communication

Game 1 – Suggest phrases or non verbal signs to be used in game. For example:

- Pointing a finger to where you want the ball.
- Shouting 'ball 'clearly when you want the ball.

Make the phrases and/or non verbal signs a condition of the performance.

Game 2 – Nominate a performer to encourage other performers. For example:

- Shouting to get back into defence.
- Positive statements when a performer makes a mistake.
- Using a positive approach – 'Good', 'Better'

Make this nominated performer use this type of communication as a condition of the performance.

Game 3 – Reinforce positive communication skills, especially when performance is not going your way. All performers have to use different types of positive communication during the activity, e.g.

- Well done!
- Clapping
- High Five!

Make using positive communication a condition of the performance.

Make the link

Communication will be vital when examining the roles and responsibilities of performers during tactics within the physical factor or within the social factor, when considering group dynamics. Without effective communication your role within your performance will be reduced.

Individual tips for communication

Set up some time to consider the following tips for effective communication. Discuss in groups the various types of communication, as well as how best to use the tips.

1. Try to use 'I' statements rather than 'you', so that the person you are speaking to does not feel as if they are being accused of something.
2. Think before you speak! Always try to speak slowly.
3. When you don't understand something, always ask!
4. Use your voice tone to highlight any important point.
5. If using non verbal communication, make sure you pay attention to whether the other person has understood or not.
6. Be clear and concise on what you are trying to communicate.
7. Be constructive on any points given.

Benefits of using these approaches

These drills are helpful because they allow the performer to experiment with different types of communication. This should mean that the links between players is more established in a real live performance situation and therefore communication should be automatic.

Limitations of using these approaches

The drills are rehearsing only parts of performance and unless they are then practised in conditioned games, it is likely they will not be used effectively once the pressures of a live performance come into play.

Interesting fact

In the sport of curling, the 'Skip' uses hand signals to communicate and to direct the next player where to send their stone.

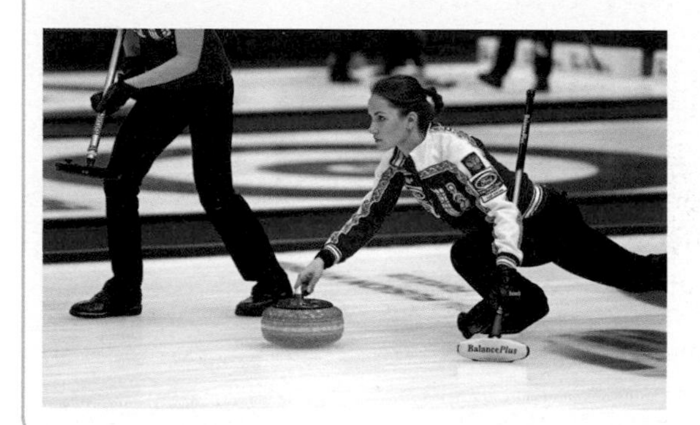

Assessment in PE

1.3 Explaining approaches to develop performance based on these evaluations.

Explaining the use of these drills within an overall development plan to develop communication would enable you to achieve this assessment standard. You would need to make clear how improved verbal and/or non verbal communication had impacted your group or team's performance.

Skills for life, learning and work

In many walks of life you will be required to communicate in a written or verbal form. You will also become accustomed to the non verbal cues of those around you. These will help you respond appropriately in a range of different situations.

Check your progress

	HELP NEEDED	GETTING THERE	CONFIDENT
1. Describe 2 types of communication.			

Advice from marker – What are the main features of these types of communication? Where and when are they used in the performance situation?

2. Explain the benefits of communication within a team or group.

Advice from marker – Give details about how relationships are affected by communication and how understanding about roles within a team are strengthened when communication is effective. Also explain the positive impact on a team's/group's performance when everyone is communicating and no-one feels isolated.

3. Describe a communication drill.

Advice from marker – What does the drill look like, how is it organised, who stands where, who does what and how is it started and finished?

4. Describe the advantages of using a conditioned game to develop communication within a team.

Advice from marker – Give reasons why this approach might work for activities you know and are familiar with. What impact do these types of games have on the live performance situation?

5. Explain one issue that might affect performance within a group/team in relation to gender.

Advice from marker – Try to give details about how girls and boys might feel when taking part in a mixed activity. Give details about the sorts of things that can cause problems as the performance is taking place.

6. Explain the advantages of working on your own when developing performance.

Advice from marker – Outline positives about having personal responsibility for what you do and when you do it. Also give details about preferences you might have in relation to training times, use of music as a motivator and how this might influence someone else trying to fit into your training regime.

8 Approaches to develop the physical factor

In this chapter you will learn how the following features can impact positively and negatively on performance:

- Anaerobic endurance
- Power
- Consistency
- Creativity
- Communication
- Role-related demands
- Team/group strengths and weaknesses

What should I already know?

You will have covered a range of physical features as part of your National 4 or 5 courses. At Higher you will look at other features, or the same ones, in more depth and develop an appreciation of their influence in performance. You will learn how to apply this knowledge to different performance contexts.

The physical factor is divided into **fitness**, **skills and tactics** and **composition**. During the Higher course, you will discover many different approaches to develop your performance within the physical factor.

Fitness: anaerobic endurance

Anaerobic endurance is your ability to work without oxygen during short bursts of exercise. It is particularly important for team sports or individual activities that require speed.

Being able to work 'without oxygen' during short bursts of intensive activity will allow the performer to use strength and speed efficiently.

Approaches to develop anaerobic endurance

Two approaches that you can use to develop anaerobic endurance are **interval training** and **acceleration sprinting drills**.

Interval training

Interval training involves working with short bursts of speed, at a high intensity, followed by rest periods. During interval training you will work both anaerobically and aerobically: you need to work with periods of high intensity, followed by rest time, which will require your body to work with and without oxygen. The principles below give you an overview of what you have to consider when planning your interval training:

1. Short intervals (10–30 seconds).
2. Long intervals (2–3 minutes).
3. Recovery – apply according to the interval phase. Short intervals – 60 second rest. Long intervals – up to 2 minutes rest.
4. Number of repetitions.
5. Frequency of the interval training sessions (normally a rest of 48 hours between sessions is required so that the body can recover after high intensity work).
6. Warm-up and cool down.

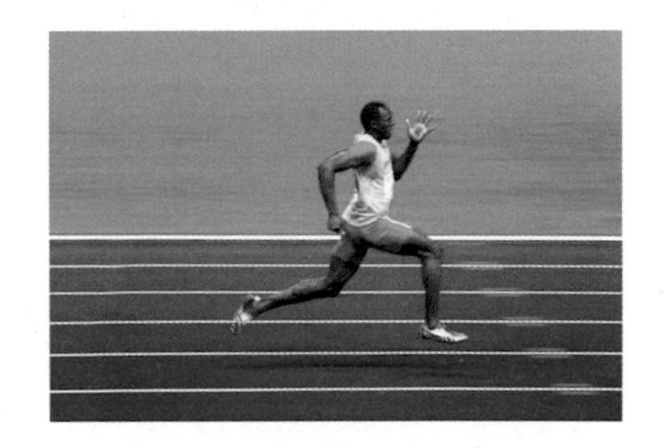

Activity 8.1

Design an interval training session using the information above to help you. An example has been given below.

Interval	Recovery	Repetitions	Intensity
Short – 20 metre sprint	10 secs	6	80–100% MHR

Benefits of using this approach

- You can adapt your interval training session easily, by increasing repetitions and decreasing your rest periods.
- You are able to progress your interval training to improve your anaerobic endurance, by increasing the intensity during the work phase.
- It will increase your anaerobic efficiency, which builds up when you are working at a high intensity.
- It will help you tolerate the accumulation of lactic acid.
- It will help you improve your speed and performance, by increasing your anaerobic capacity.

Limitations of using this approach

- Interval training can be tiring and if it is unspecific can be boring.
- Performers require a great deal of self-motivation to regularly work through intense interval training sessions.

Sprinting drills

Another approach to develop your anaerobic endurance would be to set up different sprinting exercises. Below are some examples.

Resistance drills: parachute sprinting

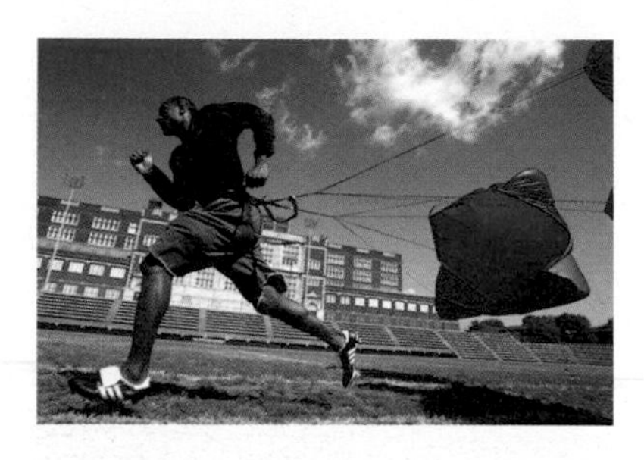

This is where you attach a parachute, which creates resistance, and try to run at top speed over a short distance. This type of sprinting drill is beneficial, as it increases your power and develops your ability to accelerate to reach your potential speed. You will need to apply your interval training principles, as discussed on page 139, when devising a session.

Benefits of using this approach

- The resistance from the parachute develops your acceleration.
- It develops speed but also leg strength.
- It is a different type of training, which adds variety to your approach.
- It is easy to add progressive overload by adding more reps or sets.

Limitations of using this approach

Special equipment would obviously be needed for this type of training. This can be costly. Also, an appropriate space would need to be found where this activity could be carried out safely. Again, for some performers this might be an issue.

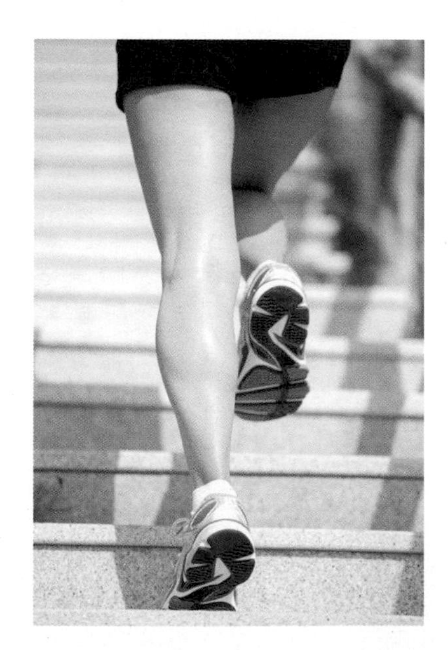

Stair drills

There are a variety of stair drills that you can incorporate into your approach to develop anaerobic endurance. For example:

- Run up every single stair, making sure you do not miss any, and then walk down.
- Place both feet on each step, making sure you do not miss any, and then walk down.

Benefits of using this approach

- No equipment is required.
- Easy to set up and complete.
- Different exercises (two are mentioned above) can be used, which can add variety to your approach.

- The steps act as resistance, which helps to develop your strength and acceleration.
- It is easy to add progressive overload by adding more reps or sets.

Limitations of using this approach

Safety might be a concern when completing this type of training. The surface and types of stairs would need to be checked carefully to ensure there is no debris and that the training could be undertaken with no risk of injury.

Hill sprints

Completing a set of hill sprints will add resistance to your sprint training, especially in the initial stages. Here is an example that you can add to your training approach:

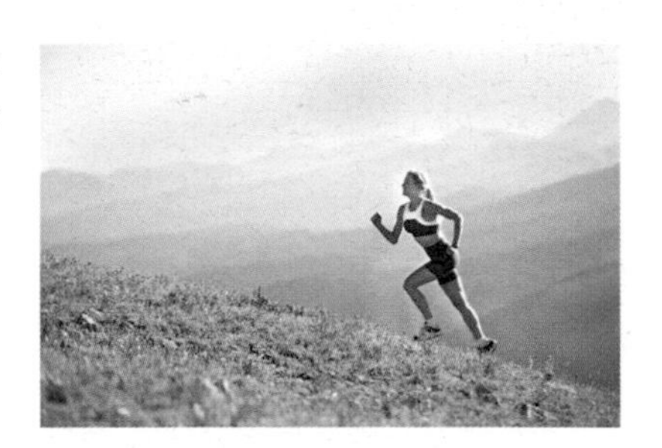

- Use a steep (no more than 15 metres), short hill.
- Sprint up the hill and walk down.
- Repeat 5 times.
- Take a 5 minute rest and repeat.

Benefits of using this approach

- No equipment is required.
- It strengthens all leg muscles.
- You can increase the intensity of your sessions by adding more sprints.
- You can add a resistance easily, through running up the hill.
- Resistance is applied straight away from the standing still position to where you have to accelerate, for example from a flat surface directly to a steep hill.

Limitations of using this approach

Again the area used to complete this type of training would need to be located. In some areas this might be difficult – inner city areas for example.

Fitness: explosive power

Power is your ability to use speed and strength in combination to improve your performance. Explosive power can impact a performer's ability to exert maximum force as quickly as possible. A variety of performers will require explosive power: for sprinting, bounding, kicking, pushing and hitting.

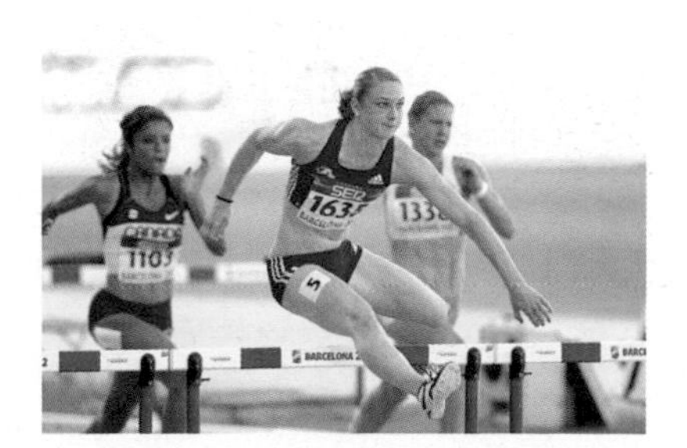

One approach to develop power is **plyometrics**, which are high intensity bounding exercises that help to increase both strength and speed of movement.

Approaches to develop explosive power

Plyometrics

Plyometrics are bounding, hopping and jumping exercises that develop speed and strength by inducing explosive reaction movements.

Exercise: Drop jumping

Description: Involves dropping down from a height and immediately spring-jumping back up. There should be limited contact with the ground before jumping back upwards. You should jump quickly and gain as much height as possible.

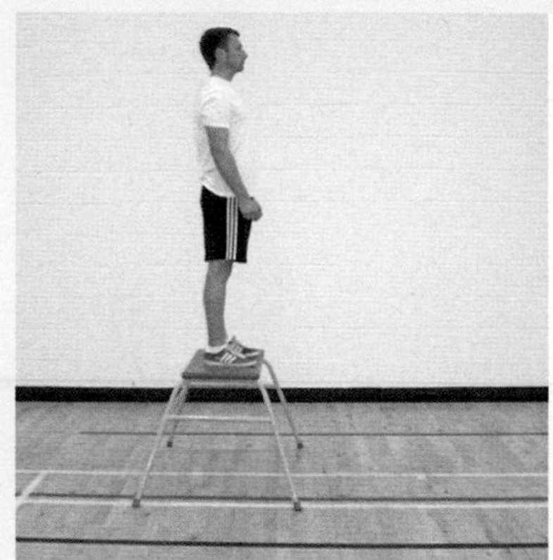

Exercise: Bounding

Description: Using long strides, you bound (form of running action, where you spend more time in the air) over a specific distance. Repeats this distance 10 times then rest and repeat another set. Different varieties of bounding can be used, such as two-legged bounds and bounding on an inclined hill, etc.

Exercise: Hurdling

Description: Set out five low hurdles about half a metre apart. Jump with both feet over the first hurdle, land on two feet and move directly over the next hurdles continuously. Keep your knees soft on landing. Walk back. Complete 3 reps, rest and complete a further 2 sets.

The height of the hurdle can be changed to add extra intensity.

Benefits of using this approach

- It combines both speed and strength approaches to training.
- It mimics some of the movements that may be used in a performance.
- It turns your strength into speed, by the explosive actions required.

Limitations of using this approach

As plyometrics is a very intense form of training and demands that the muscles are stretched again when they are at full stretch, injury can occur. Care must be taken to ensure performers are confident and aware of exactly what to do when taking part in the various exercises. This will minimise the possibility of injury.

Ballistics

Ballistics training is a form of power training that uses fast movements to project an object or your body into the air. It develops explosive power and enhances acceleration. It works your fast-twitch muscles, which in turn allows you to perform movements faster.

Some examples are outlined below.

Exercise: Explosive medicine ball throw

Description: Hold the medicine ball into chest. Lie back on a bench. Push the medicine ball into the air directly above chest. Release the medicine ball for your partner/coach/teacher to catch. Your partner/coach/teacher then places the ball back into your hands.

Set and reps: 5 x reps, rest for 2 mins, repeat 2 sets

(continued)

Exercise: Jump squats

Description: Stand with feet shoulder width apart and knees bent. Jump upwards into the air, focusing on the acceleration phase. Land with soft knees and repeat as per reps and sets. If required, you can add a weight to increase resistance.

Set and reps: 10 x reps, rest for 2 mins, repeat 2 sets

Benefits of using this approach

- Works specifically on increasing explosive power, helping to produce faster and stronger movements.
- Easy to set up and complete.
- Training allows the performer to concentrate on the accelerate phase. This is where you release the piece of equipment in a throw or the explosive action in a jump.

Limitations of using this approach

- As the intensity of this approach is high, injury is possible.
- The correct technique for each exercise must be clearly explained and understood by the performer in order that the correct technique is carried out and risk of injury is avoided.

Assessment in PE

1.3 Explaining approaches to performance development based on these evaluations

You will achieve this standard by explaining how a performer might use these approaches to understand and plan for the anaerobic and power demands of an activity.

Interesting fact

Harrison Barnes is credited with having the best vertical jump in the NBA in 2012. He reportedly jumped 38 inches (96.5cm).

Skills: approaches to develop consistency

Consistency is the ability to reproduce performances that do not vary.

Within the physical factor you will look at how skills are developed and affected by consistency. Consistency is required in all areas of performance.

The requirement for consistency affects all four factors.

Factor area	Required for:
Emotional	To stay in control of emotions for the whole performance
Social	To work effectively with others or in isolation for the whole performance
Physical (fitness)	To retain high levels of fitness throughout the entire performance
Physical (skills)	To repeat skills to same high level for the entire performance
Physical (tactics and composition)	To fulfil duties within a game plan or compositional style or form throughout a creative activity
Mental	To remain focused for whole performance

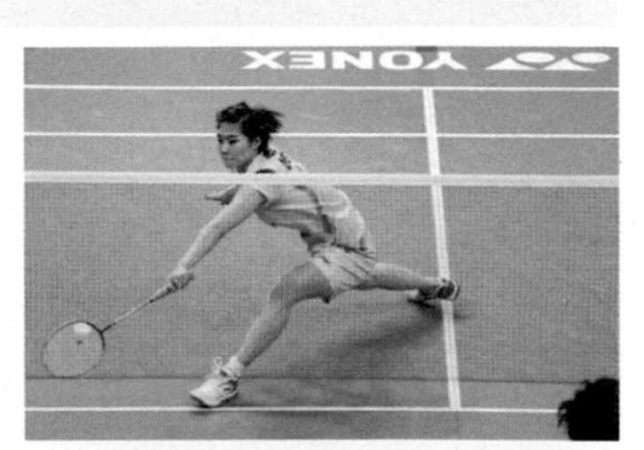

This means that, when you begin a performance, you are equipped with the correct skills and fitness demands, mental and emotional skills and an appreciation of what is involved in your role and in dealing with others around you. This enables you to be fairly certain of the results you should get.

How does inconsistency impact on performance?

Any inconsistency is penalised in some activities. For example, in gymnastics and trampolining, you have one opportunity to execute your skill correctly and are judged on it. Imagine, in basketball, if after failing a lay-up attempt your game was over and you were substituted.

Consistency in different activities means:

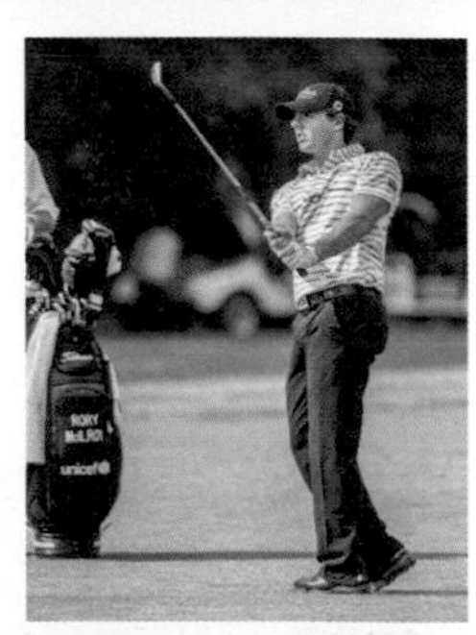

Activity	Consistency ensures a performer is:
Badminton	Able to make the serve go where she wants it to go throughout the whole match
Dance	Able to keep the quality of movements to the same standard throughout the whole dance
Netball	Able to pass accurately throughout the whole match
Basketball	Able to shoot successfully throughout the whole match
Football	Able to tackle successfully throughout the whole match
Swimming	Able to retain appropriate technique throughout the whole race
Golf	Able to stay under par as he goes round the course as one bad shot can ruin the score
Volleyball	Able to dig the first pass to the setter for the entire match

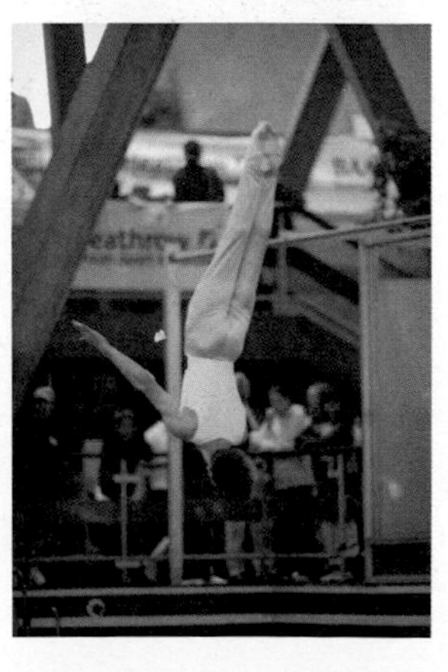

Activity 8.2

Identify the skills in your course activities where consistency is required.

Complete a graphic organiser to show the causes and effects of consistency, or lack of it.

Here is an example:

Activity: basketball

Skill: rebounding

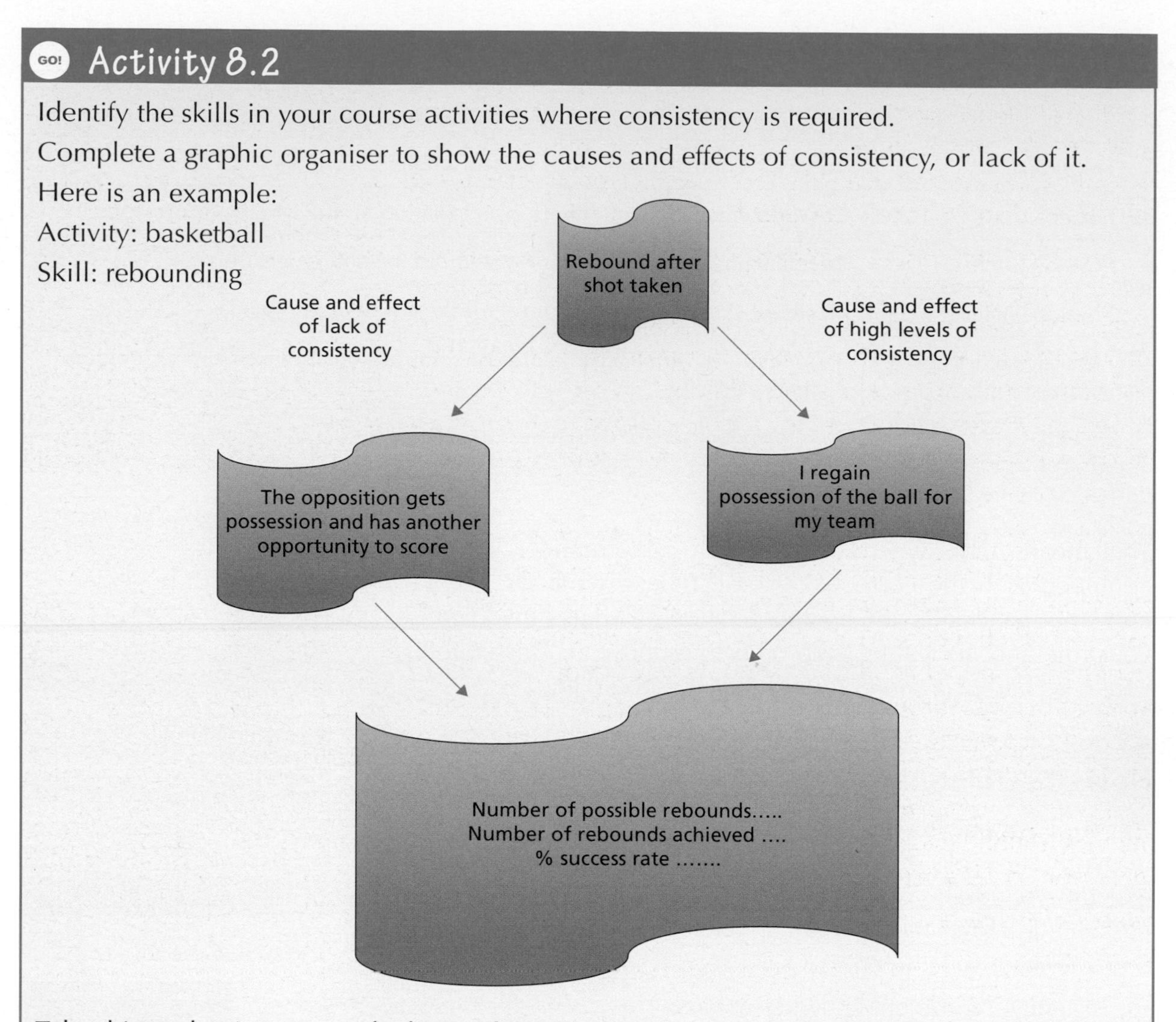

Take this evaluation a stage further and give the number of times (**quantify**) in a match you fail to gain possession of the rebound. Present this figure to support your understanding of **how much** of a problem this lack of consistency causes you.

Assessment in PE

1.2 Evaluating the impact of positive and negative factors on a performance

By being able to evaluate the impact of lack of consistency on your performance, you will be able to achieve this assessment standard.

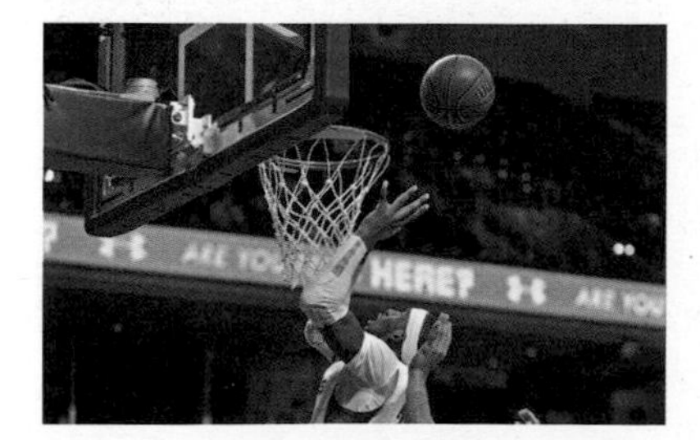

How does consistency impact on performance?

It would be wise to understand the impact consistency has on a performer. You will be able to recall times when performances went to plan – when you were able to fulfil your duties time after time without making mistakes. This consistency 'breeds' confidence in yourself and in others around you. Therefore, if you are performing alongside others it is likely your overall group performance will improve. A consistent performer is a positive influence on their group or team. She encourages others to work hard and to strive for consistency. This improves group dynamics and increases the likelihood of everyone contributing during the performance – the **social** factor.

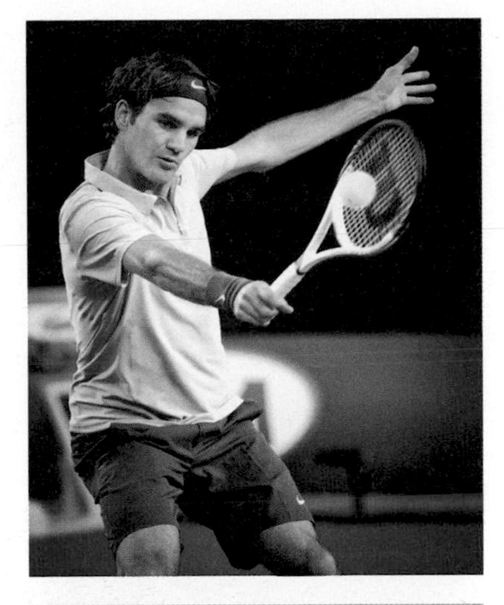

A consistent performer is intimidating to a fellow competitor. The very high level of consistency in his game often intimidated players who had to play against Roger Federer. His service was almost 94% accurate in his games; he made very few errors on his backhand and could place the ball close to the line consistently throughout games. Opponents were put off by having to play against this 'machine' that hardly ever made mistakes or displayed inconsistency.

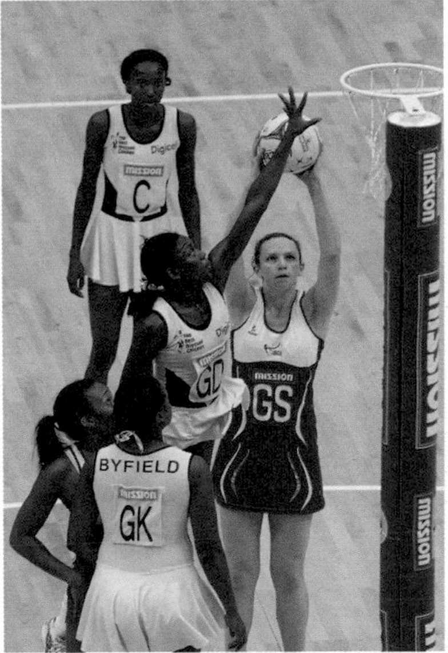

An opponent who can shoot consistently from the three-point line is very difficult to deal with in defence. A goal attack who can score from anywhere in the circle when she receives the ball is a real challenge to a goal defence. The defender's lack of consistency in being able to stop her shooting can make motivation levels drop, cause errors to be made and even affect self-control levels as she gets frustrated while trying to put her off. The goal attack on the other hand feels confident, in control of the match, empowered and unstoppable, which increases her motivation levels, reduces the mistakes she makes and increases her ability to be positive and determined.

Success depends on consistency and consistency ensures success.

Approaches to develop skill consistency

In this section we are focusing on developing consistency of skill during performance.

To develop a skill we must first identify which **type** of skill it is.

An open skill is one that is affected by the conditions under which it has to be used. This means it might be performed differently each time it is used. For example:

- pass in rugby
- tackle in hockey
- shot in handball
- overhead clear in badminton.

> **Make the link**
>
> For consistency in terms of emotions, mental skills or physical fitness, look at approaches suggested in the other chapters of this book.

A closed skill is one that is dictated by the performer entirely. That means it is done the same way each time. It is largely unaffected by what is going on around the performer. For example:

- service in badminton
- diving.

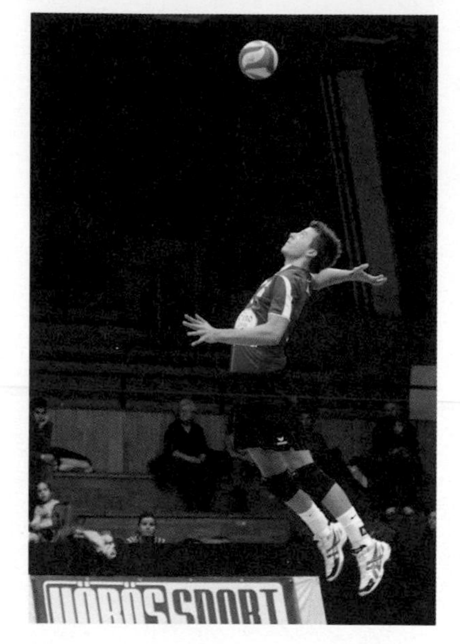

The **type** of skill you choose to focus on will affect the approach you use when trying to develop consistency.

We will look at three different approaches to develop consistency.

Approach 1: blocked approach

This approach is particularly useful when working on the consistency of a closed skill. The performer would repeatedly use the **identical** technique over and over again to perform the skill with the **same** outcome or goal each time.

Here is a description of the blocked approach used to develop the serve for volleyball.

Stage 1

Identify a target area for the service to land. Mark this out on the opposite court. In the early stages this will need to be quite large to allow for errors in consistency.

Stage 2

Focus on the throw up of the ball and ensure it is correct before hitting the ball. If the throw up is not consistent, then the service is unlikely to be so. If the position of the ball is not correct, do not hit the service; let the ball fall to the ground.

Stage 3

Hit 20 serves and ensure a partner records the landing position.

Benefits of using this approach

This approach allows the technique to be repeated exactly the same way each time. It does not ask for or require any adjustments to the technique and allows the performer to repeat the movements over and over again.

When the correct technique is repeated over and over again, a strong muscle memory trail is created in the brain. This requires the performer to watch where the service has landed and reflect on how it felt when he served. This should be done uninterrupted to allow the performer to **link** the correct techniques to the successful outcome of the skill.

That is – did the technique produce the correct result?

When this feedback is received by the performer it enables him to see instantly how consistently successful the technique was. That is, if only 8 out of the 20 land in the target area, it would be accurate to assume that consistency has not yet developed.

The performer then works towards knowing when the correct technique has produced the correct outcome. He would use his **kinaesthetic awareness** – internal feedback – about what it felt like to be able to recognise when he had produced the correct technique. The hope is that by understanding what has to be done to achieve success, it can be replicated. This means consistency is more likely.

Limitations of using this approach

The blocked approach used in training can be repetitive and boring. It would be necessary to introduce targets and feedback to ensure a performer stayed motivated while working to improve performance.

Approach 2: variable approach

A variable approach to develop the same volleyball service would only be possible once the technique was fairly automatic and there was some degree of consistency. By introducing this variability into training, the skill can be practised under more realistic game-like conditions.

Stage 1

Repeat the serve to different target players who will change position before receipt of service.

Stage 2

Record the success of the serve to the various targets.

Benefits of using this approach

This approach encourages slight modification of the technique when being used. This makes it more likely for the skill to be transferred into a real, live performance environment following the use of the variable approach.

The use of different target players replicates the demands under which the service would need to be used in a game. That is, the server would not want the service to always go to the same place, as the receiving team could easily pick it up. Also, the server would want to be able to pick out a weaker passer in the opposition team to target, in the hope that he would not play a good first pass to the setter, or in fact not pick up the service at all. A performer would most likely be at the associative stage of learning when using this approach. This would be because they had gained some experience of the skill and would be able to achieve a degree of success. In the earlier stage of learning (cognitive stage), many mistakes are evident as the performer is still developing muscle memory associated with the skill.

Limitations of using this approach

It is a challenge to be able to set up to use this approach within performances that are realistic. Again this might be fairly repetitive and boring if variety is not included.

Approach 3: random approach for use with open skills

This approach demands different skills to be linked together. In volleyball, for example, it would be used to develop consistency of passing from the service. The player would be encouraged to move, ready to receive a pass. As soon as the first pass is played, another skill is then added on. This means that the number of skills used increases. The variety of different random plays should allow the performer to experience the different types of responses she must cope with within the demands of the performance situation.

Stage 1

Serve is received and played to the setter. Success or otherwise is recorded.

Stage 2

Serve is received and played to the setter and then performer must move to spike the ball over. Success of service reception is recorded.

Stage 3

Serve is received and played to the setter, who then plays it straight over so the performer has to immediately jump to block the failed set. Success of service reception is recorded.

Benefits of using this approach

This random approach is useful because it mimics the kinds of phases of play that can happen within the overall performance and the different responses that are required.

In testing out these responses in practice, long-term memory trails are established and the performer is able to recall these more consistently during performance when required. That is, the more exposure she gets to the types of situations that might occur, the more likely it is that she will be able to do the right thing more often in a game = consistency.

Limitations of using this approach

This approach demands more complex thinking, i.e. while playing the performer needs to think about what comes next, as well as the other things she needs to do and where she should move to.

This is only possible when a performer is at the autonomous stage of learning. This is because by now she can perform the skill with a high degree of success without having to think about **how** to play it. Consistency is developed as a by-product because game-like scenarios are used.

Assessment in PE

1.3 Explaining approaches to performance development based on these evaluations

By explaining why these approaches might be used to develop skills, you will be able to achieve this assessment standard.

Implementing these approaches within a development plan

When developing these techniques for use in any activity an awareness of the stage of learning and the type of skill is required. This would ensure you chose the most appropriate approach to develop the skill. Your focus would obviously not just be restricted to improving the technique, but also to ensuring the skill could be used consistently and effectively throughout a whole performance.

Therefore, while working through the blocked, variable or random approaches, the number of successful attempts would need to be recorded. This would ensure the correct techniques were being used consistently throughout.

This would also allow you to evaluate if the approaches had been successful in improving your consistency. The percentage increase in the number of successful first passes would be a clear indication that your consistency levels had increased.

Assessment in PE

2.4 Evaluating the effectiveness of the development plan and the methods used to monitor development

By being able to produce evidence of the success of the approaches you used in terms of quantity of successful first passes, tackles, serves or shots on goal you would be able to achieve this assessment standard.

2.5 Identifying and justifying decisions relating to future personal development needs

Justifying the need to continue training for consistency would help you achieve this assessment standard. Performers who strive to be consistent are more likely to see continued improvement. Learning while performing, as well as practising, will ensure that different performance demands are analysed and so skills are 'fit for purpose'. This means that, after performing, analysis of consistency levels would be required in order to ensure that execution of skills remained at a high level. Overall performance would then improve.

Skills: approaches to develop creativity

Some people say creativity is inherent – that you are born with it. Others say that once a basic skills repertoire is taught, creativity can be developed.

Creativity in physical activity is:

'Characterized by originality of thought; having or showing imagination.'

Collins English Dictionary

One thing most teachers and coaches agree on is that creativity can only be nurtured if the conditions or environment are right. This means that if a performer feels it is acceptable to try to do something creative then he or she will.

Take a look at this video on YouTube:

http://www.youtube.com/watch?v=AQpAcgpnHnk

In this clip Wayne Rooney talks about having tried a spectacularly creative shooting technique in the past and how it failed. A creative player like Rooney has the confidence to try using skills and techniques that might not be successful. Researcher Gregory Feist looked at how creativity affected performance and noted that those with high levels of creativity were:

- very self-confident
- impulsive and determined
- less affected by what others thought of them
- very focused on the role they had to carry out.

Creativity can be exemplified by looking at this continuum:

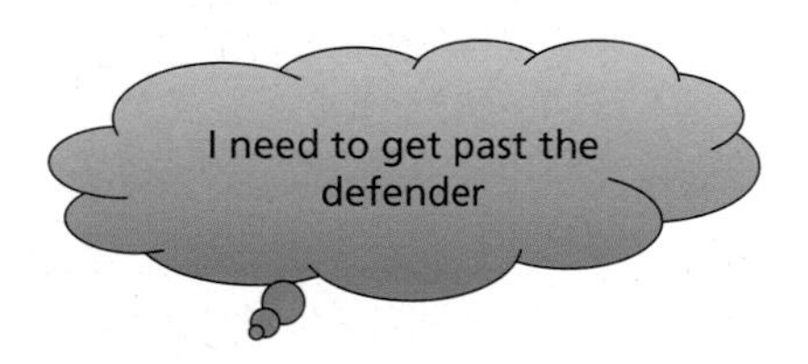

Thought process of performer with low levels of creativity

Thought process of performer with high levels of creativity

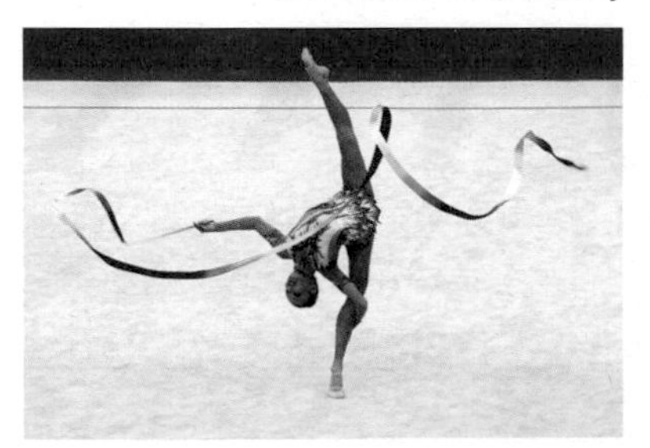

Having high levels of creativity in activities would allow you to:

- trick or deceive an opponent
- make a dance, gymnastics or trampolining sequence look interesting and unusual.

Divergent thinking

This involves an element of **divergent thinking**, where the performer would see more than one solution to a performance problem during a performance.

In terms of creative activities, this would mean planning a sequence where different linking skills would be included or techniques used with a variety of changes of direction and/or levels.

In team or individual games, the performer would try to use variation and disguise to take control of the game and make it difficult for the opposition to anticipate what they were going to do. This would win points or increase the opportunity for goals to be scored. In this way creativity would have a very positive influence on performance.

Lack of creativity in any performance would mean that it would be predictable and uninteresting. This could result in an audience becoming bored or fewer points being awarded for creativity or artistry within a sports 'acro' competition. In this way creativity would limit the performance.

FLOOR

	Connection Values											Content = top 8 values	Composition Reqs @0.5 each	
FLOOR	Indirect	C+D	0.1	C+E	0.2	Acro Direct	B+D	0.1	A/B+E	0.2		including the dismount	1 180° lp series	4 BAx2 +360°
				D+D	0.2		C+C	0.1	C+D	0.2			2 Acro Ln 2 saltos	5 C dismount 0.3
		A+A+D	0.1	A+A+E	0.2		A+A+D	0.1				Max 5 Acro Min 3 Dance	3 Salto F/S +Bkwd	D dismount 0.5
	Salto/Jump	D + A	0.1									All Falls = 1.0	short Exercise	
Artistry	Creative Choreography ~ 0.3			Express music/idea 0.1			Variety rhythm & Tempo 0.1				M&M 0.3		Background music 0.5	mimics/ gesture 0.1
Specific	> jump/Lp/Hp to prone 0.1			Low level move 0.1			Turn on 1 foot 0.3					no attempt dsmt 0.5	M&M at end 0.1	Excess prep/Pause 0.1

180 series		DIFFICULTY				DV		
Acro 2 saltos			Ac	Da	Total	CR		
Salto F/S+ Bk		G .7				CV		
BAx2+360		F .6				D Score		
DMT		E .5						
		D .4				E Score		
		C .3						
		B .2				Final Score		
Execution	Artistry	A.1						

180 series		DIFFICULTY				DV		
Acro 2 saltos			Ac	Da	Total	CR		
Salto F/S+ Bk		G .7				CV		
BAx2+360		F .6				D Score		
DMT		E .5						
		D .4				E Score		
		C .3						
		B .2				Final Score		
Execution	Artistry	A.1						

180 series		DIFFICULTY				DV		
Acro 2 saltos			Ac	Da	Total	CR		
Salto F/S+ Bk		G .7				CV		
BAx2+360		F .6				D Score		
DMT		E .5						
		D .4				E Score		
		C .3						
		B .2				Final Score		
Execution	Artistry	A.1						

FLOOR

LR June 09

GO! Activity 8.3

Watch this clip and identify the points the commentator makes about the need for creativity in this interesting activity.
http://www.youtube.com/watch?v=CtwrFaJtsZQ

Assessment in PE

1.2 Evaluating the impact of positive and negative factors on a performance

By being able to show clearly how creativity impacts on performance, you will be able to achieve this assessment standard.

Approaches to develop creativity

Gradual build-up approach

Building creativity depends on the performer's stage of learning. At the cognitive stage of learning, it is unlikely that creativity would be a focus for the performer. At this stage, many mistakes are made and linking between discrete skills would be simple and uncomplicated.

For example, a simple sequence of:

tuck ⟶ straddle ⟶ pike ⟶ seat drop

might be completed. However, as the performer became more confident with these simple skills, half turns could be added to take the performer into the skill or added as the skill was completed. This would add to the overall creativity of the sequence.

By using the **gradual build-up approach**, the performer could gradually add in more complex, interesting variations to the sequence.

In dance, a simple 16-count motif could be made more creative by adding a change of level or a spin. Again this would ensure the dance was more engaging to the audience.

When using this approach within creative activities, the choreographic/development process will require the performer to be encouraged to try the new, more creative links, while being supported where necessary or even with positive feedback to ensure the performer feels confident. This will maximise the chances of the correct motivation levels being present. Adding a new, more challenging part to a sequence is often very hard work and can be discouraging. However, once a more creative part has been mastered it can be very rewarding.

Benefits of using this approach

A basic level of skill is required before creativity is possible. Gradual build-up allows elements of a sequence to be changed or adapted or skills to be used in different ways. By gradually and slowly adding more complex links into a sequence it can look more creative and interesting. Or using a simple change of foot or hand with the ball can mean an opponent is tricked into believing the player is going in one direction instead of the other.

Limitations of using this approach

Progress can be slow when learners are at an early stage. This can be demotivating and performers may be tempted to use variations of a skill before they have actually achieved a high enough level of consistency and competence with a skill.

Improvisation approach

Improvisation is another approach that can aid the development of creativity. A performer might be given lots of opportunities to add new parts, moves or skills to a sequence in practice sessions, which might result in new, exciting, innovative and creative pieces of work. This improvisation approach builds in the conditions for a performer to feel confident when trying out a variety of options or solutions – without the fear of ridicule or failure. This is how the process works. Often the failed or unsuccessful attempts can be modified or adapted to add a more unusual element to the performance.

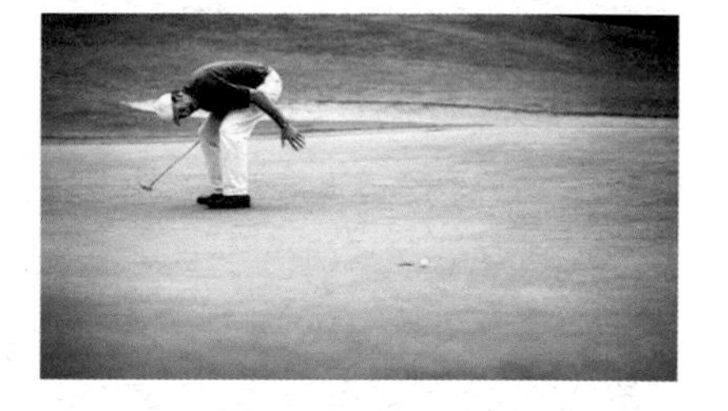

In games or sports, creativity can be developed using this same principle of allowing faults to be made. Even the most creative of sports-men and women make mistakes. However, the clever thing is that they are able to store these failed attempts and retain high levels of confidence so that they might have another go and risk failing again.

Wayne Rooney's attempt at the halfway line shot in the example given earlier in this chapter shows how a creative player never loses the confidence to try again with something that might succeed on a second or even tenth attempt!

To develop creativity in a player, divergent thinking has to be encouraged. Therefore the type of approach used must provide the opportunity for the player to see the types of performance problems that might arise and to investigate, try out and evaluate the success of a variety of solutions that are possible.

> GO! **Activity 8.4**
>
> In this clip below, the player with the ball HAD to be creative as he had no other player to support him. https://www.youtube.com/watch?v=xPtvyumUOb8
>
> 
>
> Analyse what the player who scored the goal did to make it difficult for the players who were trying to get the ball from him.

Benefits of using this approach

Belief in a performer's creative ability is a wonderful characteristic to encourage. This means an element of the unexpected might occur. Spectators might witness a more interesting and engaging performance when the performer is confident to try something different and interesting.

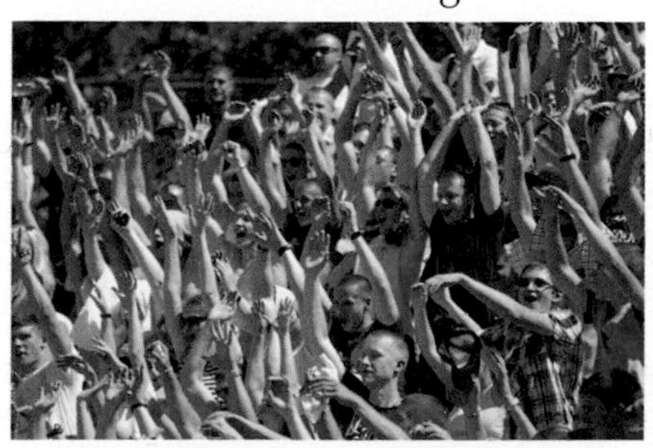

Limitations of using this approach

Most performers want to be creative. However, a performer who keeps trying to do something different or creative in a dangerous situation can end up losing points or goals. The most creative gymnastic moves are often the most dangerous.

Activity 8.5

Watch this clip https://www.youtube.com/watch?v=NZ7rFUB1PjM

Discuss the advantages of a performer wanting to add in more complex and possibly dangerous skills into their repertoire.

The scenario approach

A **scenario approach** can be used to develop creativity. This approach sets out a performance problem and allows the performer time to consider what the options might be. Then, through practical application of these solutions, the success and appropriateness of the options chosen can be considered.

The scenarios begin with familiar performance problems, moving to more challenging, unfamiliar situations. The purpose is to allow the performer to be creative, to build his armoury of skills, confidence and practical possibilities which can be used to deal with the performance problem.

A simple hockey example would be for a teacher to set up for a player to try to shoot around a cone positioned at the edge of the box.

Once the player has gathered experience on where the ball should be struck and how much power is needed in order to beat the goalkeeper, the scenario can be further developed.

The next part of the scenario that could be introduced is the presence of a two man 'wall'. The options the performer now has are affected by the addition of players who, although passive, are in the way of a clear shot at goal.

The options could be discussed with the performer or she could be left to solve the problem by trying a variety of solutions she has in her armoury. There is no pressure to score, the defenders will not add to the pressure to 'get the shot off' at this stage and everything the performer tries will allow some time for reflection about what was appropriate or successful.

The next stage would be to make the defenders 'active'. They must now close down the shooter as she comes towards them. The performer is encouraged to try to be creative, to do something the defenders do not expect.

This encourages the performer to watch the defenders, to try to ascertain which side is their strongest, where the goalkeeper is standing, what space is available around the defenders and if she can play the ball around the wall, or knock the ball to the side to run onto.

What she sees will affect what she decides to do.

This scenario approach will take the performer through a process which moves the thinking from:

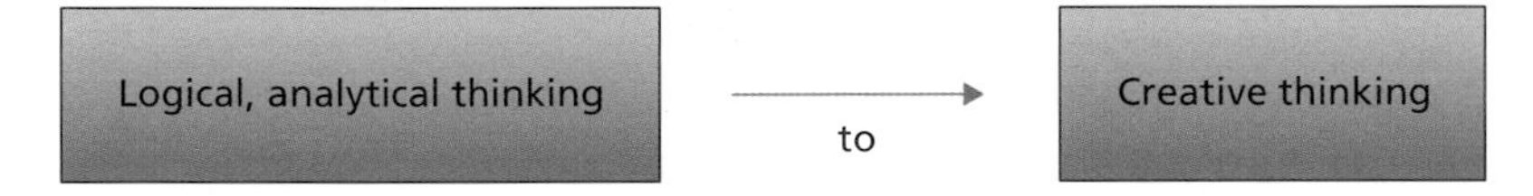

In the scenario approach, trying and then failing is regarded as necessary and a teacher or coach would never stifle (prevent) this attempt to grow creativity.

In basketball a number of plays might be rehearsed in training. Although each player has set places to move to and set cues that indicate when this movement should take place, the opportunity for a player to be creative and do something unexpected must also be allowed. This might mean setting aside some time for individual players to have the opportunity to adapt or modify their part in the play. This would allow the team to rehearse and experience a range of different outcomes for some of the set plays.

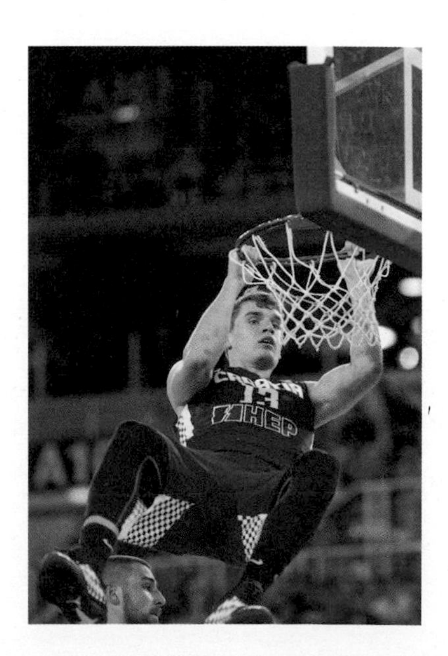

By encouraging players to take risks, and try out adaptations of learned patterns or plays, an opposition can be completely split apart. This climate of spontaneity will encourage players to:

- think creatively
- be unafraid of trying something new or different
- be confident in their own ability
- feel sure they can deal with the opposition.

What is tried in training will then be transferred to the live game by players who are confident they have permission and the ability to be creative.

Benefits of using this approach

By manufacturing environments where different scenarios are created to encourage creativity, performers are exposed to the variety of responses that can be made to any given performance problem. This means in the live performance, creativity should 'flow'.

Limitations of using this approach

Lots of time needs to be set aside in order to set up this type of training environment. This can reduce time needed for other aspects of performance development.

Assessment in PE

1.3 Explaining approaches to performance development based on these evaluations

By explaining how these approaches can be used within a development plan to develop creativity you will achieve this assessment standard.

The inclusion of these approaches within a programme of work to develop this feature would ensure high quality performance overall. Skill development, fitness and tactical training must include an element of creativity training if a performance is to be successful at a high level.

Creative activities require by their very nature – creativity. Without creativity in games, predictability is present. Players then depend on errors from the opposition.

Creativity development should be built into a development plan for the **whole** performance where, once skills were mastered, tactics or compositional elements would be agreed and practised or rehearsed. Creativity considerations would be regular, probably during every session and would be entirely matched to the performer's role, with clear targets and goals for development agreed. These principles of effective practice would ensure the approach used was effective in developing this feature of performance.

Skills for life, learning and work

Creativity and consistency are desirable qualities in many jobs. Being able to create something different in the field of marketing or information technology, for example, makes an employee very valuable. Also being able to always produce high quality work consistently means you can be trusted to carry out important tasks.

Tactics: role-related demands

In every activity you have a role to carry out. For example:

- Dance – soloist
- Badminton – individual player
- Football – centre midfield
- Netball – goal defence
- Hockey – sweeper
- Gymnastics – individual performer
- Basketball – guard

The role the performer has to fulfil in any of these activities is dependent on the performance context, i.e. the type of activity. There are many different types of activities, but for our purposes we will group activities into seven different categories:

1. Games
    - Target games – where the purpose is to hit an object to a target, e.g. golf.
    - Net/wall games – where the purpose is to hit a ball or shuttle into an area on the opponents' court where it cannot be returned, e.g. volleyball.
    - Striking/fielding activities – where hitting and catching a ball is required, e.g. cricket, softball.
    - Invasion games – where the purpose is to attack a goal or target, e.g. football, basketball, rugby or hockey.
2. Athletics
3. Gymnastics
4. Dance
5. Outdoor pursuits
6. Combat sports
7. Swimming or water-based activities

Within these categories activities are also:

- Directly competitive, i.e. what your fellow competitor does has a direct impact on what you are required to do. For example, tennis – the opponent forces you to move to the right-hand side of the court to return the ball.
- Indirectly competitive, i.e. competition is still happening but you can carry out your performance entirely unaffected by what your fellow competitor does. For example, swimming – as you swim in a race you can ignore (if you choose) that the swimmer in the next lane is increasing his stroke rate towards the end of the race. Or, in gymnastics, one gymnast performs after another.
- Non-competitive, i.e. activities that are done outwith a competitive environment, e.g. walking or cycling.

Of course, an activity can also be either a team/group activity or an individual activity.

GO! Activity 8.6

Make a performance catalogue of all the activities you know by placing them in the correct category. You should note that some might fit into more than one category. An example has been given.

Activity	Type	Individual or group/team	Example
Swimming	Non-competitive	Individual	Swimming for leisure or fitness
Swimming	Competitive	Team	4 x 50 m relay
Swimming	Competitive	Individual	400 m butterfly

Role-related demands of individual activities

The type of activity will dictate the roles that are available within it. For example, in individual activities, a performer does not have a position to carry out, as they would in a basketball team. However, they have duties associated with their role as an individual performer.

In dance, for example, the soloist needs to:

- Position herself in her starting position to ensure the music starts on cue.
- Stay in time with the music.
- React and adjust to any bad landings or movements that take her out of time with the music.

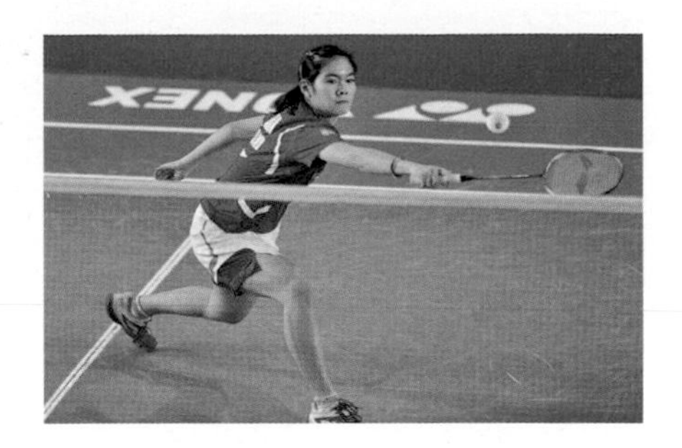

In badminton singles, the player needs to decide:

- Which serve to use.
- When to use his overhead clear to build an attack.
- When to smash.
- When to use disguise.

A long jumper is responsible for:

- Measuring and marking his run-up.
- Beginning his warm-up before his jumps.
- Getting himself prepared mentally for the event.
- Making adjustments to run up during the competition.

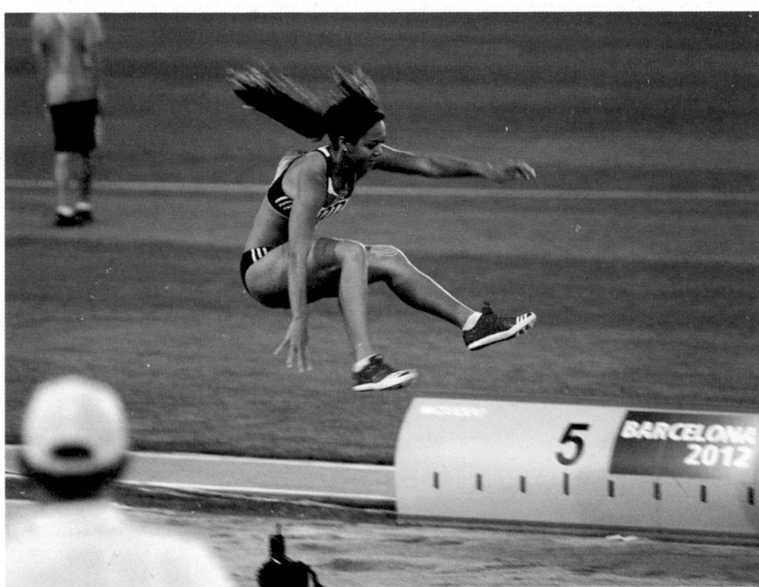

Role-related demands of team activities

Within team games, roles are more defined. For example, goal defence in netball, spiker or libero in volleyball or a goal keeper in football.

In addition to your duties and responsibilities as the performer, it is possible you will have other roles within your group or team. For example, as captain you will be required to help organise the team while they play, keep everyone focused and give feedback where necessary in order that the team works together as a unit.

You must identify and understand the role-related demands that you must fulfil within your performance. Role-related demands are those tasks you need to do before you begin your performance, during the performance and sometimes after the performance.

A graphic organiser would help to make this clear.

GO! Activity 8.7

Identify the role-related demands within your performance.

Here is an example of a graphic organiser for a captain in a netball team:

Before game:

- Positions agreed
- Team warm-up carried out
- Centre pass coin toss completed
- Motivate and encourage teammates to get match focused during warm-up

During game:

- Encourage defenders
- Change tactic for centre pass
- Pass on instructions from the coach
- Keep team focused at all times

After game:

- Thank umpire
- Organise 3 cheers
- Get the team together for a summary/debrief on how the game went
- Organise and ensure a thorough cool down

Here is another example for a setter in volleyball:

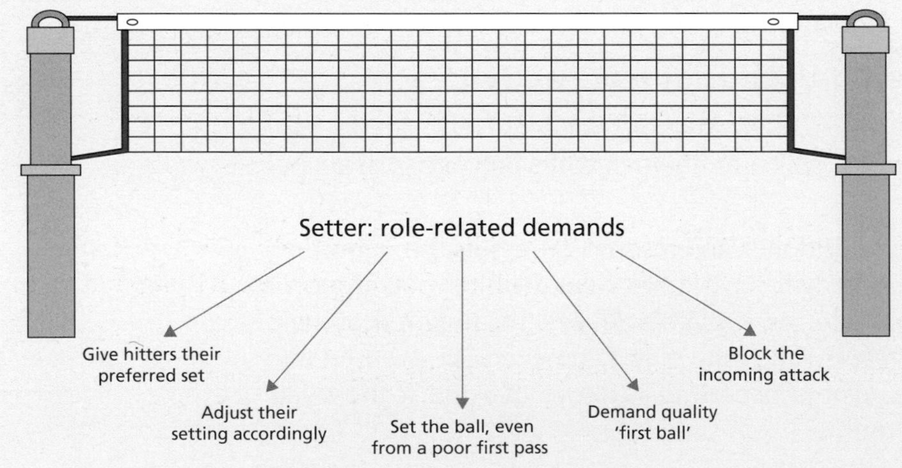

Role-related demands within different strategies or formations

Once these demands are clear and understood, you should also investigate the demands of your role within different strategies or formations.

For example, the role-related demands of being part of a group performing a jazz dance would require all dancers to be able to use specific types of techniques and styles.

Within the fast break, a guard's role would be to receive the outlet pass and begin the drive towards the opposing basket.

Therefore, identifying the types of formations you use within your activity would be required in order to agree what the role-related demands are for each position or role.

A formation is an agreed way of covering the playing area/performance area with the group or team. In dance, this might be to have a pyramid shape, as shown below.

1
2 3 4
5 6 7

Once the formation is decided, players/performers are allocated a role that has specific demands associated with it. The role allocated should match the performer's ability and skills. For example, a centre midfielder will often be the strongest, fittest player in a hockey team, as they are expected to be constantly supporting the attack and defence.

Activity 8.8

Draw out any formation you use in activities from your course using the example above to help you.

GO!

Activity 8.9

Identify the specific requirements of a role within an activity from your course, as has been done in the example above.

These might be:

- Physical requirements, e.g. fast, strong, tall, high skill level.
- Mental requirements, e.g. effective decision-maker when under pressure.
- Emotional requirements, e.g. high levels of self-control.
- Social requirements, e.g. excellent team contributor.

Approaches to develop role-related demands

Finding approaches to assist in the development of these roles can be quite challenging. However, there are certain approaches that can be applied to developing any role within a performance.

Integrated approach

In a team/group activity, the approaches you use to develop a skill or an aspect of fitness could also bring about improvements in how you deal with role-related demands. This might mean using an **integrated approach**.

This approach would match up fitness requirements, skill requirements or mental or emotional requirements into one development plan.

For example, a centre back player might use approaches designed to develop an understanding of role-related responsibilities alongside work to develop cue recognition (mental factor). Therefore, a programme of work might be designed using a variable approach (skills – physical factor) to develop a player's ability to function effectively as part of a flat-back-four defensive structure. The conditioned game would allow the use of conditions that meant wave after wave of attacks had to be dealt with by four defenders, while keeping their structure and fulfilling their duties to stay goal side of the approaching strikers and to move to 'jockey' or cover when appropriate. Cue perception would be developed at the same time, where a coach or other players would be calling out instructions to 'watch' or to cover. This is known as the **peer support recognition approach**.

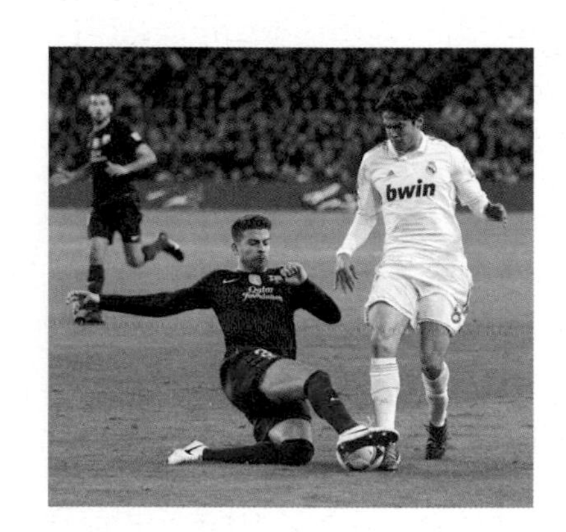

The performer is therefore integrating two approaches – **conditioned games** and **peer support recognition** – into one integrated development plan.

Benefits of using this approach

Developing the role that a performer has at the same time as developing the skills or tactical knowledge required is quite straightforward. For example it would make sense to work with a player on their hit out of defence in hockey **because** they need to clear the ball from the danger of an impending attack. The sweeper would learn that in this situation he must use his strong hit to make safe the defensive area he is protecting.

Limitations of using this approach

In a training or practice situation it is possible to reinforce and encourage players to carry out their role effectively at the same time as using the appropriate skills required. However, in a live performance context this gives the inexperienced performer a lot to think about. This can sometimes cause problems when they either don't have the skills to carry out the role effectively or they don't understand what they are required to do in the role they are playing.

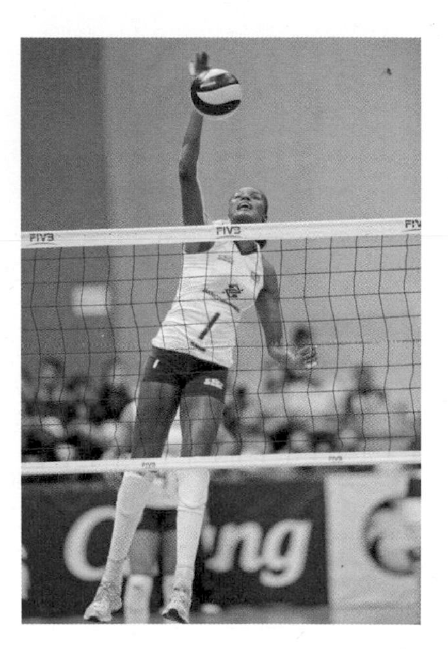

Gradual build-up approach

Another approach that can be used to help develop role-related demands is **gradual build-up**. This involves gradually increasing the complexity of the demands of the skill. For example, when learning the spike, you might start with spiking against the wall to get the technique right, then from a hand feed, then from a volley from a setter and then after a first pass and the set.

Within the area of strategies, formations and/or composition, the **gradual build-up approach** can be utilised.

When dealing with the demands of a specific role within a strategy, there is a very clear, straightforward **gradual build-up approach**.

Stage 1

The demands of the role (position) are explained to the performer. This will give visual pictures and diagrams to illustrate where on court the different role-related responsibilities are carried out. This includes:

- Where to stand
- Where to play
- Which skills to use
- What responsibilities are part of this role.

Effectively, the performer will **talk it through** with a coach or other group member to make sure they understand it.

↓

Stage 2

The performer gets the chance to **walk it through**. This includes:

- Watching a model performer carry out the described role.
- In a small-sided version of the activity, the performer gets the chance to try out the role and, with coaching throughout, attempt to modify parts of the performance where required.
- This walk through is done at a slow pace, with little pressure, no defence if possible and where the result is unimportant. Feedback is constant and stops and starts are allowed during which the performer can go back to stage 1 if clarification about the role-related demands is required.

↓

(continued)

Stage 3

The player gets many chances to repeat at game pace and succeed while performing the role-related demands of the strategy. Again, feedback, discussion and **talking it through** might still be needed.

↓

Stage 4

Passive defenders are added in to increase the pressure on the performer to carry out the role-related demands under more game-like pressure. These defenders will apply pressure simply by their very presence on court. They will move towards the player with the ball, but will not attempt interception or dispossession. Again, feedback is a feature of this stage and clarification is allowed when necessary.

↓

Stage 5

Active defenders are introduced. These defenders will work just as they would in a full game. When they manage to get the ball, however, the drill or game is over. This means the performer does not experience the pressure of thinking about dealing with an imminent attack from the opposition. Again clarification about role-related demands is permissible.

↓

Stage 6

A full practice game is organised where coaching is allowed to reinforce the role-related responsibilities of different performers. Unlimited time outs are allowed in order that corrections and further clarifications can be given to make sure a performer is doing what he needs to do within the performance.

Benefits of using this approach

This is a gradual, slow and supportive way for a performer to make progress while developing an understanding of their role. The performance environment can be structured to ensure more role responsibilities are added on only when the performer is ready for them.

Limitations of using this approach

It can be a slow process to develop all the skills and qualities required for each role. Also, for others involved in the performance the constant stop–starting can be very frustrating.

Analytical approach

For an individual performer, an **analytical approach** can assist the dancer, swimmer, badminton player, tennis player, rower, table tennis player, runner, jumper or thrower in dealing effectively with the role-related demands of her activity.

This approach entails systematically following a six-step process.

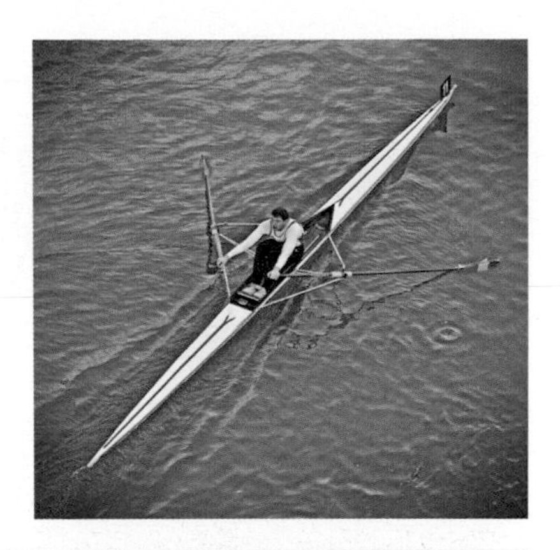

Step 1

The performer carries out clarification of the performance environment and/or conditions before starting the performance. This would include:

- playing/performance surface
- lighting, weather and surrounding performance areas.

↓

Step 2

Carry out a warm-up or rehearsal of the performance.

↓

Step 3

The performer revisits the agreed plan/tactic/choreography for the performance.

↓

Step 4

The performer is responsible for carrying out the performance plan.

↓

Step 5

The performer is responsible for adapting the plan, where necessary, while performing.

↓

Step 6

Debrief session – the performer carries out an evaluation of what went well and what might need to be changed for next performance.

Benefits of using this approach

Using this approach before, during and after the performance allows the performer to take full responsibility for all elements of the performance. Making use of this analytical approach would allow a table tennis player to progress through a tournament, a dancer to perform a number of dances as part of a dance show, a gymnast to have all three attempts at their vault or the high jumper to compete in a full competition at different heights.

The individual swimmer is completely responsible for taking her position on the starting blocks, for reacting to the starter's gun and for carrying out the race plan. Understanding the responsibilities within this role can be very positive. The swimmer should feel able to make all the decisions that affect her performance. She can feel empowered that all she needs to do is swim the race she has planned. It also means that the glory associated with a successful swim is directed towards the swimmer alone.

Runners sometimes look as if they are unaware of the other people around them. When a group splits away from the pack, spectators might feel that the runners in the trailing pack should try to catch up. However, a runner who understands the role-related demands of the activity, and has gone through the **analytical approach,** has prepared himself for the decision he must make in this very situation.

He will have prepared properly and be aware of who he is running against and what strengths and weaknesses they have. This will all have been included in his race plan. Even if this has been prepared with the aid of a coach, on the day, in the race, only the performer himself can take the decisions required while the race is happening.

The role demands that the performer watches for a group breaking away and also watches the lap times to ensure the pace is as planned.

In the cycling time trials at the Glasgow Commonwealth games, Alex Dowsett of England was almost 6 seconds behind the leader. However, a steady and well thought out race plan saw him pull back in the last section to win the gold medal.

Limitations of using this approach

More negatively, however, an individual athlete can feel so much pressure to fulfil the demands of the role that he 'chokes' when he needs to be absolutely in control. This can be because there is **so** much to think about. Being focused on lap times, stride patterns and lane positions in order to be in the right position and condition to make a move when required, in a very stressful performance situation, can mean athletes are unable to carry out their role effectively.

Assessment in PE

1.2 Evaluating the impact of positive and negative factors on a performance

By being able to evaluate the impact of the demands of your role, both positive and negative, you will achieve this assessment standard.

The **analytical approach** instils in the athlete the need to be aware of required adaptations if a group moves away. The final stage of this approach (the debrief) adds to the 'database' of previous race results available to the athlete, which they can then use to help them decide whether to go with the break-away group or continue at the rate planned before the race.

Assessment in PE

1.3 Explaining approaches to performance development based on these evaluations

By explaining how a performer might use these approaches to help understand and plan for the role-related demands of an activity you will achieve this standard.

Tactics: team/group strengths and weaknesses

In this section we will look at how strengths and weaknesses within a team/group can impact performance and some possible approaches to deal with some of these strengths and weaknesses.

Not all activities have teams, but for our purposes the terms 'team' and 'group' will be interchangeable.

In team or group activities the aim is to get everyone working together towards a common goal, i.e. winning! If everyone pulls together to carry out their role effectively, then the dynamic between performers is likely to be positive.

There is an old saying:

'A team is only as strong as its weakest player.'

Make the link

Group dynamics

The feature 'group dynamics' lies within the social factor. Within any development plan you organise, you may want to look at this feature in order to make sure relationships are strong and positive within any group you participate in. This is known as group/team cohesion.

As you work through the strengths and weaknesses of groups/teams you will deepen your understanding of how performance can be positively and negatively affected by group cohesion.

Activity 8.10

Research and present a graphic organiser showing an example of when the strongest/best players were not chosen in a starting line-up.

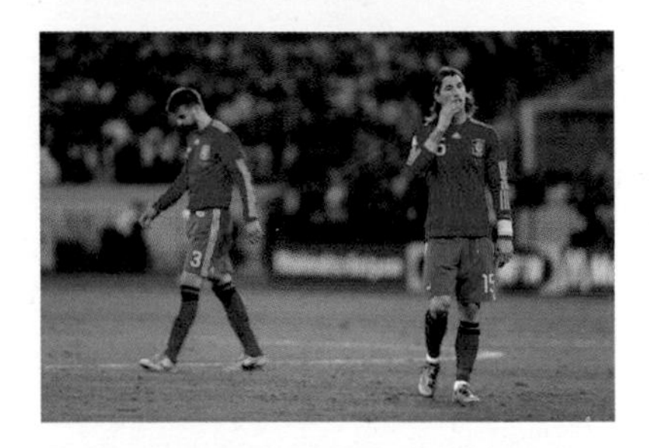

Activity 8.11

Look at:

http://news.bbc.co.uk/sport1/hi/olympics_2004/basketball/3567344.stm and http://www.youtube.com/watch?v=sdeuZPE3uCA

Draw up a chart to give possible examples in the game when the team had not worked together efficiently.

Clip 1

Clip 2

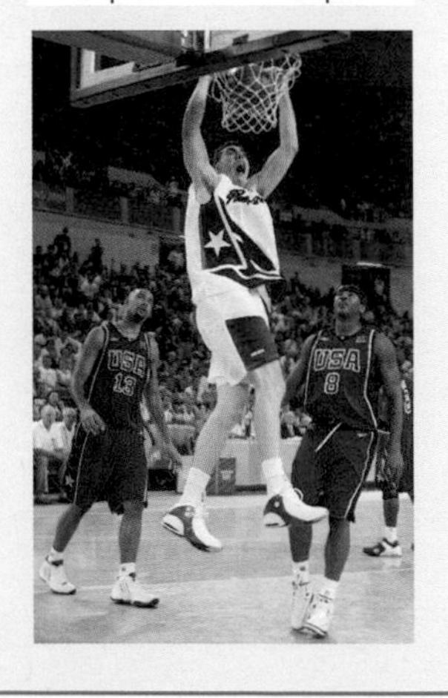

This means that everyone in a team can impact the success of a performance and so all strengths and weaknesses need to be taken into account when planning for a successful outcome. Indeed, there are some instances where a coach might put on a player who is less competent in order that their positive work ethic influences the whole team.

In some competitions the best players are brought together to form a team with the aim of winning, e.g. World Cup football. The eleven 'superstars' who make up the squad all have the skills, experience and confidence to dominate any opposition. However, there are instances where these components are not enough. For example, in the 2010 World Cup, Spain had lost only one game in the previous four years and was deemed very likely to do well in the whole competition. However, the team suffered a shock defeat against the much lower rated Switzerland, losing 1–0. They did recover after this game to go on and win the tournament having learned a very good lesson about working together as a team.

Another example is when the mighty USA basketball team were beaten 73–92 by underdogs Puerto Rico in the 2004 Olympics. In all interviews the American team's coach could offer no real explanation of what had gone wrong except to say that the team had not managed to work effectively together.

Interesting fact

Most international teams now have specialists working with them to develop positive team spirit. The men's Great Britain hockey squad spent two nights on Dartmoor with specialist army squadrons working together to overcome tiredness and poor conditions in an attempt to build positive relationships and team identity.

Strengths and weakness of a group or team

In team or group activities, the strengths and weaknesses of the group are vital considerations when performing. If a team is able to identify a strategy that makes best use of the performance strengths of the individuals within the team or group, then it will be more likely to succeed.

In a performance context, this would mean that the group would make use of key players at particular times during a game and, as the performance went on, grow in confidence and motivation. For example, putting the tallest player in the goalkeeper position against an equally tall goal shooter may mean that she manages many interceptions and allows the team to move up court and score.

A team might be considerably weakened by ignoring the strengths of individual players. Players without the necessary skills might be placed in positions where they are ill equipped to deal with the responsibilities required of them. For example, a less experienced hooker comes off the bench in an important match. The first thing he has to do is throw in at a line-out 5 metres from his own try line. The mental skills, emotional skills and physical skills of this player are all going to be tested right from the first second he comes on the pitch.

A team or group that is not aware of its weaknesses would be disastrous, with group members being asked to carry out roles or use skills that they do not have. As in the example above, this might leave a team exposed to attack from the opposition.

Assessment in PE

1.2 Evaluating the impact of positive and negative factors on a performance

By explaining how the strengths and weaknesses of your particular team or group affect your performance, you will be able to achieve this assessment standard.

Teams and groups are made up of individuals who have their own strengths and weaknesses. Knowledge of these strengths and weaknesses are used when planning a strategy, formation or choreography to make use of the team or group's strengths and to minimise the potential problems an individual performer's weakness might create.

Strengths and weaknesses of the opposition

It is also important to be aware of the strengths and weaknesses of the opposition.

In preparation for the Wimbledon Championships 2013, which Andy Murray won, Ivan Lendl, his coach, watched video footage of all possible opponents he might meet throughout the tournament. Together they planned a specific strategy for each match and opponent. For example, the type and preferred angle of serve Murray would come across were discussed and so Murray went into the game knowing what he should do when faced with a 'big server'. The motto: 'Fail to prepare, prepare to

fail' was certainly in Murray's mind as he went forward into the most successful time of his career. He had obviously decided to leave nothing to chance.

A swimmer would be wise to know the strengths of the opposition as he goes into a race. This allows him to be prepared for his main competitor's fast start, even paced mid race and sprint finish. Being prepared in this way allows the swimmer to focus on his own race while being aware of what others around him might do.

A badminton doubles pair would be able to anticipate the strengths of their competitors from previous competitions. This would give them some assistance when planning their own strategy for the game. If one of the players was less fit than the other, the plan would centre around making this player move around the court in order to tire her out and force mistakes.

Knowledge related to the strengths and weaknesses of any opposing group or team would be an advantage. This would allow you to try to counteract their plans and make it difficult for them to dominate or to achieve their best performance.

Approaches to develop team/group strengths and deal with weaknesses

The matching approach

In some sports, a **matching approach** is used. This involves matching the abilities or qualities of players in a team with players in an opposing team – for example, a tall player marking a tall player. Effectively there is an attempt to match strengths and weaknesses.

If a group ignored this approach then **mismatches** would occur. This could mean a fast player has a slower opponent. In terms of any attack, overload would occur very quickly and goals or points would be conceded, as a team would exploit this mismatch.

Mismatches can take various forms:

- Players can be mismatched in terms of physical fitness.
- Players can be mismatched in terms of physical size or body type.
- Players can be mismatched in terms of mental ability.
- Players can be mismatched in terms of emotional stability.
- Players can be mismatched in terms of social features, such as fair play.

Therefore, when planning to improve performance, considering your own team's strengths and weaknesses and how these match the strengths and weaknesses of the opposition, could help you maximise your chances of doing well. Prior knowledge and experience of the opposition needs to be taken into account but, even where this is not possible, changes that respond to the opposition's unforeseen strengths or weakness can be made during time-outs and by substituting players.

GO! Activity 8.12

Go to the website:
http://eplindex.com/30756/do-substitutes-win-games-stats-analysis.html

This site attempts to show the impact substitutions have on goals scored when managers make changes during a match.

A skilled performer can see mismatches and exploit them during play. For example, when a right-handed player is faced with dribbling past a strong left-handed player, the decision she makes about which side to pass her on will be crucial. As the play continues, each player should be building a library of observations relating to the types of things an opposition can or cannot deal with. The plan would be to pressurise them into doing the things they can't deal with and to stop them doing the things they can deal with.

Therefore, in doubles badminton, the players would force their opponents to play shuttles that travel down the middle of the court as they stand side-by-side because this leads to indecision and confusion. Similarly, in the same scenario, there would be a planned tactic to ensure the stronger of the two players was not given the opportunity to smash, as this would be an area of strength for him.

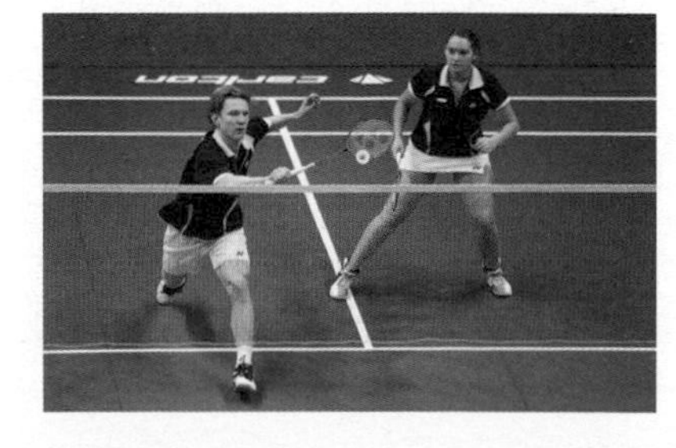

All players need to be able to evaluate the strengths and weaknesses of opponents. This allows them to make use of their own strengths and to exploit parts of the opponent's game to their own advantage.

Benefits of using this approach

By matching players' abilities it means a team can minimise the impact individual strengths can have on a performance. It means too that competition will be tight and players will have to work hard throughout the game.

Limitations of using this approach

It is not always possible to match the individual strengths of an opposing team. This might mean a team has to compromise by setting players up as best they can. There might still be some mismatches but the team will have to go ahead and start the game anyway. This can lead to demotivation and poor team spirit as a team struggles to cope with opposition players dominating play.

Playing to strengths and avoiding weaknesses

Knowledge about the demands of the competition or performance environment allows the performer to **play to his own strengths while avoiding or hiding his weaknesses**. This approach can be applied in hockey, football, basketball, handball, cricket, shinty – in fact any team or individual sport.

This approach of playing to strengths and avoiding weaknesses does not ignore what the actual team or group weaknesses are. It requires detailed analysis of the strengths and development needs of the team/group. In this way a plan can be made to make maximum use of strengths and to try wherever possible to avoid or even hide weaknesses. The approach deliberately places players in certain positions and arranges dancers at certain areas of the stage in order to minimise the impact of weaknesses on the overall performance.

Within this area of the physical factor, team group strengths and weaknesses must be identified.

Once the team weaknesses are identified, a development plan using approaches from **other** factor areas might be required. This is because individuals make up a team or group and they almost certainly will have different personal strengths and development needs. These will determine which tactic/strategy or composition is used.

For example, each group/team might have a range of strengths and weaknesses in terms of:

- physical fitness
- skills
- understanding of roles within tactics or compositions
- managing emotions
- mental fitness
- ability to work effectively within a team or group.

In these cases, organising a programme of work with appropriate approaches would be the correct course of action. This means you are using knowledge and skills from the other factors that impact performance to enable you to improve the weaknesses of your team or group.

For example, when trying to improve a team or group performance as part of the physical factor, it could be identified that it was in fact the mental factor that is causing most problems. A programme of work to deal with weaknesses in anticipation might be required. This means the mental factor has an impact on this physical factor.

Look at Chapter 5: **Approaches to develop the mental factor**. Identify approaches that might be used to improve the anticipation of the whole group/team.

Assessment in PE

1.3 Explaining approaches to performance development based on these evaluations

By explaining how you would use the **matching approach and** the **playing to own strengths and avoiding own weaknesses approach** within an activity you will achieve this assessment standard.

Looking at the other factor areas to see where the emotional, physical or social factor affects the mental factor will help you make connections across the four areas.

For example:

If the weakness was a player losing his temper when facing a stronger opponent, then an approach could be **parking**. (Emotional Factor, anger: self-control, page 102.)

If the weakness was that individuals in a team dribbled the ball forward in attack instead of passing early to another player in a better position, then a possible approach could be **team communication drills**. This would enable the team to work through training scenarios during coached games. (Social Factor: communication, page 134.)

If the weakness identified was a problem with the execution of a particular skill, then a possible approach might be **the variable approach**. (See Physical Factor, skill: consistency, page 144.)

If the weakness was the inability of a player to carry out her role because she couldn't jump high enough to block, then an approach could be **plyometrics**. (See Physical Factor, fitness: explosive power, page 141.)

If the weakness was a player not understanding what they had to do in a particular situation, then an approach might be **gradual build-up,** where she was gradually exposed to more demanding, competitive aspects of the performance within training. (Physical Factor, tactics: role-related demands, page 159.)

If the weakness was a player being unaware of a second striker running towards them, then an approach might be an **unstructured approach** to anticipation training. (Mental Factor: anticipation, page 90.)

Putting in place a development plan to improve your weaknesses as a team would require you to be specific about the aspect that needs attention.

Having identified the areas that need attention, you would work on the team strengths and weaknesses within training sessions at least once a week. Coaching would be required to ensure that the areas focused on were given enough training time.

Benefits of using these approaches

By making use of approaches from other factor areas, the link between the four areas can be seen.

Team/group strengths and weaknesses are likely to be mental, physical, emotional or social. Therefore, the approaches you may already have used for your own personal development are appropriate for teams/groups also.

Limitations of using these approaches

When a team does not train together it loses group identity. Therefore, even though individuals might prefer to work in isolation while training to develop performance, planning must take place to bring group members together to check progress, discuss new targets and try new strategies or compositions/ choreographies. It is a fine balance to allow individuals to work on their own personal weaknesses while still focusing on the needs of the overall team/group.

Make the link

Look at the social factor approaches when developing your performance within a group or team. Consider specifically if you need to use the 'buddy' approach or if you would prefer to work on your own using the 'self-focused' approach.

Assessment in PE

2.3 Implementing the development plan

By demonstrating the use of approaches to develop team/group weaknesses, you would achieve this assessment standard.

Data collection would then be repeated to see if the areas that had been highlighted as problems had been improved. You would expect to see improved:

- Statistics of fewer players losing their temper when facing a stronger opponent using the **parking approach**.
- Consistency in the execution of particular skills after using the **variable approach**.
- Ability of a player to carry out their role because she can now effectively jump to block after using the **plyometrics** approach.
- Understanding of what had to be done in a particular situation through the use of the **gradual build-up** approach, where players were gradually exposed to more demanding, competitive aspects of the performance within training.
- Awareness of a second striker running forwards through the use of an **unstructured approach** to anticipation training.
- Evidence of individuals within the team passing early to another player in a better position through the use of **team communication drills**. This enabled the team to work through training scenarios during coached games.

The same principles apply to creative team/group activities. A group of dancers would need to identify which part of the choreography the group was struggling with. Then they might decide to:

- Use gradual build-up if the weakness was in the linking of different motifs together.
- Use a circuit training approach if local muscular endurance was a problem for the group.
- Rehearse the dance with success imagery to increase confidence and improve recall of the steps.
- Use centering to improve the group's ability to handle pressure from the presence of an audience.

By using statistics, questionnaires, self-reflection sheets and coach feedback to prove that performance has improved, you can demonstrate the impact your development plan has had on your performance.

Assessment in PE

2.4 Evaluating the effectiveness of the development plan and the methods used to monitor development

By trying to quantify **how much** your performance has improved after carrying out your performance development plan, you will achieve this assessment standard. You should also give judgments about qualitative evidence you have gathered that shows your overall performance could be assessed as having improved. You must also show that you have evaluated how useful your methods of monitoring progress were.

Evidence generated by comparing performance before and after the implementation of a development plan will enable you to evaluate:

- If players are more consistent and how many more times they were consistent in the execution of skill.
- How many more times a blocker was able to jump within a game.
- How many players were more successful in dealing with the demands of a particular situation in a competitive context.
- How many more times players passed early when participating in the fast break instead of dribbling ahead themselves.
- If there were fewer instances of players losing their temper within the competitive environment.

Check your progress

	HELP NEEDED	GETTING THERE	CONFIDENT
1. Explain the possible attraction of working on your own when developing performance.			

Advice from marker – Give details about why you might prefer to work on your own when training. Your answer therefore must include statements like 'I like working on my own because...'

	HELP NEEDED	GETTING THERE	CONFIDENT
2. Evaluate the benefits of using the improvisation approach when you begin working to improve performance.			

Advice from marker – Give details about the value of going through the process and being encouraged to think during the different scenarios you were in.

	HELP NEEDED	GETTING THERE	CONFIDENT
3. Describe a performance where you made use of your strengths to achieve success within your performance.			

Advice from marker – Give details of what the performance looked like, what you did well, who played where, what did the dance/swim/jump feel like?

	HELP NEEDED	GETTING THERE	CONFIDENT
4. Explain why it would be necessary to hide or avoid weaknesses within a performance.			

Advice from marker – Explain what would happen if you had to use a stroke that you knew was poor, or what happened when you had to put a player in a position that she had never played before.

	HELP NEEDED	GETTING THERE	CONFIDENT
5. Justify why it would be helpful to exploit an opposition's weaknesses in a competition.			

Advice from marker – Make a case for playing the ball to a weak backhand in badminton – what would it allow you to do?

	HELP NEEDED	GETTING THERE	CONFIDENT
6. Explain why creativity makes an activity **look** more interesting.			

Advice from marker – Give details about how much more interesting, varied, unusual or unexpected a creative performance can look.

	HELP NEEDED	GETTING THERE	CONFIDENT
7. Research some creative performers. Describe what makes their performance more creative for you.			

Advice from marker – Give details about things they do, how different they are to others in their 'field'.

	HELP NEEDED	GETTING THERE	CONFIDENT
8. Explain why allowing performers to experiment within different scenarios encourages creativity.			

Advice from marker – Give details of how allowing opportunities for performers to try different responses, moves or steps without fear of failure encourages new confidence to try unexpected, more interesting and varied things.

	HELP NEEDED	GETTING THERE	CONFIDENT
9. Describe how you would make use of an integrated approach to develop two features within this factor.			

Advice from marker – Describe how each training session would be organised to allow the performer to focus on two different features. Use the suggested integrated training programmes in the appendix at the back of the book to prompt you to think about how your whole performance training was organised.

	HELP NEEDED	GETTING THERE	CONFIDENT
10. Explain why each stage is necessary in the gradual build-up approach when developing a performer's understanding of their role.			

Advice from marker – Give step-by-step details of **why** each stage gets more demanding, why it gets progressively more challenging and game-like.

	HELP NEEDED	GETTING THERE	CONFIDENT
11. Describe the principles of training for developing any aspect of physical fitness.			

Advice from marker – Describe what SPORT means.

CASCO
MacLEAN

Monitoring and evaluating

9 Monitoring and evaluating

In this chapter you will learn:

1. How to monitor your performance.
2. How to make comparisons before and after performance.
3. Why monitoring is appropriate.
4. Evaluating your performance after performance development.

What should I already know?

During the National 5 course, you will have developed an understanding of how and why monitoring and evaluation can be used to enhance your performance development. At Higher level you will be required to show you understand the purpose behind monitoring and evaluating and how these would be carried out and used to inform changes to the work you carried out to improve performance.

Assessment in PE

2.4 Evaluating the effectiveness of the development plan and the methods used to monitor development

By being able to draw conclusions about how successful your development plan was and to make judgements about the usefulness of the methods you used to help you monitor the process, you will achieve the assessment standard.

Below are examples of how you may wish to monitor your performance development. It is crucial that you understand this monitoring process and how it is fundamental to your performance development, so that you are able to prepare for and complete your assessments in the unit and the exam.

Monitoring methods

Training diary

One of the main methods of monitoring your performance will be taking notes on your performance development in a training diary. The next table gives some examples from a training diary and shows how this information can be used.

Date	Extracts from diary	How to use the information
14/3/14	Found the interval training quite easy to complete. Managed to complete 3 x 200 m in 45 seconds quite easily. Then repeated.	• What decisions and changes do I need to make in my training programme? • Is my performance still improving?
16/3/14	Decreased the time taken to complete my interval training to 40 seconds, which made the training more challenging.	• How will this affect my training?
25/3/14	Athletics meet. Did not manage to reduce my time for my 400 m. Still felt I was tiring toward the 300 m mark. Pretty disappointed.	• Has the approach had a positive or negative impact? • How can I motivate myself?

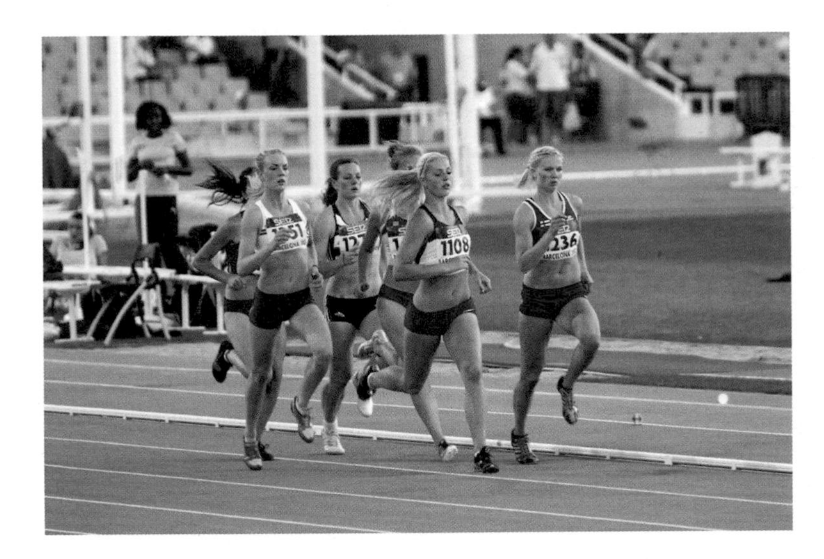

Within your training diary you will be able to take notes about your performance development across all four factors. You may find that one factor can have a direct impact on another, or perhaps you have found you have been able to develop more than one factor at the same time. Keeping a training diary will allow you to have all this information at hand.

Repeating data collection

Another essential part of monitoring the performance development process is repeating the same data collection methods before and after performance development. This enables accurate comparisons and conclusions to be drawn about the effectiveness of the approaches used.

For example, to monitor your aerobic endurance, you could compare the data collected from two time-related observation schedules.

Time-related observation schedule 1: Completed on 13/3/14

	Time in performance			
Skill level	0–5 mins	5–10 mins	10–15 mins	15–20 mins
Dribbling at speed	✔	✔	✔	✖
Passing	✔	✔	✔	✖
Shooting	✔	✔	✖	✖
Receiving pass	✔	✔	✔	✖
Movement patterns	0–5 mins	5–10 mins	10–15 mins	15–20 mins
Marking	✔	✔	✖	✖
Moving into space at speed	✔	✔	✖	✖
Tracking opponent at speed	✔	✔	✖	✖
Movement in fast break	✔	✔	✖	✖

✔ = effective
✖ = not effective

Time-related observation schedule 2: Completed on 1/4/14

	Time in performance			
Skill level	0–5 mins	5–10 mins	10–15 mins	15–20 mins
Dribbling at speed	✔	✔	✔	✔
Passing	✔	✔	✔	✔
Shooting	✔	✔	✔	✖
Receiving pass	✔	✔	✔	✔
Movement patterns	0–5 mins	5–10 mins	10–15 mins	15–20 mins
Marking	✔	✔	✔	✖
Moving into space at speed	✔	✔	✔	✖
Tracking opponent at speed	✔	✔	✔	✖
Movement in fast break	✔	✔	✔	✔

✔ = effective
✖ = not effective

Activity 9.1

Using the time-related schedules on the previous page, complete the table below, which will lead you through key questions you need to ask yourself when monitoring and evaluating your aerobic endurance.

Question	Response
What data have I gained from time-related observation schedule 1?	
What data have I gained from time-related observation schedule 2?	
What key aspects in my performance have been impacted in time-related observation schedule 1?	
What key aspects in my performance have been impacted in time-related observation schedule 2?	
How will I use the data from both time-related observation schedules?	
How will this help me in my performance development?	

Extracting the key information from repeated methods of data collection should allow you to see where improvements have been made and how to plan for your future development needs. Through monitoring and evaluating your performance, you will always be seeking to improve the factors impacting your performance.

By setting up methods of monitoring and evaluating performance you will be able to gain invaluable information about your progress and your next steps in your performance development route.

Key considerations when monitoring and evaluating performance

Make sure you use up the same **protocol** each time you complete the monitoring process. It is essential that you gather information from each performance in as near to the same conditions as possible. Think about the following when setting up methods to monitor your performance:

- Use the same method of data collection.
- Try to keep conditions the same.
- If possible, use the same teammates/teacher to help you gather information.
- Be clear in what you are trying to achieve.

Keeping to the same protocol will allow you to gather more accurate and valid information. This will allow you to achieve a reliable analysis of information, which, in turn, will allow you to come to more accurate conclusions and clear and achievable next steps.

One of the key skills you will develop is your ability to make **accurate comparisons**. When making comparisons, whether through specific methods of data collection or monitoring, it is useful to ask yourself the following questions:

1. Are there any differences in the information collected?
2. Are there any similarities?
3. Can I link any of the information together?

Make the link

In other subject areas you will need to be able to draw conclusions from information. For example, in English, you may have to compare and analyse the language and techniques of two different writers. Think about the stages you need to go through to do this. Perhaps you can apply them to your monitoring and evaluating work?

Why are some methods better than others?

The methods of monitoring you decide to use will depend on many factors, for example:

- On what you are trying to gather information.
- The depth of analysis you want to achieve.
- The resources you have.
- Where the monitoring will be completed.

You need to make sure that you use the most appropriate methods to monitor your performance. For example, when monitoring your aerobic endurance, it is useful to complete two time-related observation schedules (to make comparisons) and a recognised aerobic endurance test, such as a multi-stage fitness test or the two sets of data generated by the PaceTracker app. This way you will be able to monitor your performance both within and outwith the activity. This will allow you to back up any findings and plan realistic next steps. It also provides a combination of factual (objective and quantifiable) and qualitative (subjective) information. This gives you as clear a picture as possible.

Sometimes gaining subjective information based on how you feel when performing can be particularly useful. For example, when gathering information on how emotional factors such as anxiety have impacted your performance, it is essential to consider your own personal opinion.

GO! Activity 9.2

Complete the table below by gathering information on the social factor. Imagine the types of comments that would be inserted before any approach had been decided upon. Then complete table 2 and imagine how you would feel after you have had an opportunity to develop this factor.

Personal reflection 1 (before development)

Social feature	Comment
During my performance, how did I cope when working as part of a group? Did I communicate? Was I willing to listen? Did I accept others' opinions?	
During my performance, how did I cope when working in isolation? Was I able to focus? Was I confident in my own decisions? Was I concerned about what my classmates might think?	

Personal reflection 2 (after development)

Social feature	Comment
During my performance how did I cope when working as part of a group? Did I communicate? Was I willing to listen? Did I accept others' opinions?	
During my performance how did I cope when working in isolation? Was I able to focus? Was I confident in my own decisions?	
Was I concerned about what my classmates might think?	

Now complete the following questions to help you with your analysis.

Question	Response
What data have I gained from personal reflection 1?	
What data have I gained from personal reflection 2?	
What key aspects in my performance have been impacted in personal reflection 1?	
What key aspects in my performance have been impacted in personal reflection 2?	
How will I use the data from both the personal reflections?	
How will this help me in my performance development?	

Evaluation of performance and future development needs

Evaluation

After monitoring your performance, you will need to make evaluations based on the information collected and identify any future development needs you may have.

The table below shows examples of evaluative comments based on data collected during the monitoring of the emotional, social, physical and mental factors.

The methods identified have already been explained in previous chapters.

Factor	Methods of monitoring	Evaluation of performance	Future development needs
Emotional: anxiety	**POMS test**	By revisiting my POMS test, I can make comparisons between my before and after tests and evaluate my current level of anxiety and the impact it is now having on my performance. I scored much higher in my second test, especially in the questions related to my anxiety levels. This has impacted my performance as I feel I am now much better at using coping strategies when I get really nervous, which has allowed me to perform more efficiently and effectively.	My next steps are to try and add some more pressure situations into my performance, so that I can work on developing my strategies for coping with anxiety. This would allow me to stay calm during different pressurised performance situations.
Social: working together	**Group feedback**	Through the feedback gathered from my peers, I can now recognise the times when I work well with others and when I do not. It has also allowed me to evaluate the types of situations I find myself in when I don't work well with others. This has impacted my performance, as I am now more aware of when I am in these situations and I am able to turn this around.	In the future I feel I will be more conscious of how important it is to work with others during my performance. I will be more aware of the importance of listening to other people's opinions, as well as putting my opinion across in a positive manner.
Physical: fitness	**Time-related observation schedule**	I developed approaches to increase my aerobic endurance. By repeating my time-related observation schedule, I can now see that I am able to track back during the final quarter of my performance and that my skill level is still relatively high, with 70% of my passes on target. This has a significant impact on my performance, as I am able to pass and move accurately and track my defender during the latter parts of my performance, which has allowed my team to perform more effectively.	In the future I will try to maintain my level of aerobic endurance, so that I can perform at a high intensity throughout performances. I will endeavour to build aerobic training sessions into my performance development plan, so that it is always a significant part of my training.

(continued)

Factor	Methods of monitoring	Evaluation of performance	Future development needs
Physical: skills	**Skills test before and after performance development**	Through evaluating my skills test before and after my performance development sessions, I am able to get quantitative evidence on whether the consistency of my passing has improved or not. From my second test I can see that my score in the test has increased by 20%. This has a positive impact on my performance, as I am now able to pass consistently throughout the majority of my game, allowing more attacking opportunities to be set up.	I still need to work on the consistency of my passing and this may be something that I will always need to practise. My next steps will be to set up practices that add more movement when passing and more pressure from defenders. This will allow me to practise the consistency of my pass in more game-like settings.
Physical: strategy, formation and/or composition	**Training diary**	Throughout my performances I have been keeping a training diary of my roles and responsibility. I have been able to gather information on how my role within my composition has progressed and adapted. From this I can see where the key improvements have been made.	I will continue to work on the different roles required within my composition. I may look to link this to different compositional styles, which will enhance the way in which I work with others during my performance.
Mental: controlling aggression	**Discipline record**	I have been able to look back over my disciplinary records from this season and see where, when and why my performance has dropped due to me being unable to control my anger. I used this information to try to use different strategies in my performance when I felt I was about to lose control of my temper. I found that during the second half of my season I had fewer instances recorded and felt much calmer and in control when performing.	In the future I am going to continue to work on strategies that will allow me to keep calm, even in challenging situations. This will allow me to become more of a team player.

The evaluation process allows you to use the information gathered from monitoring, analyse it and come up with key evaluative comments. You might want to ask yourself some evaluative questions, such as:

Have I improved?

Why have I improved?

What evidence do I have?

If you don't complete this process, you may continue to make the same mistakes, which will impact negatively on your development.

Future development needs

Once you have evaluated your performance, it is important that you think of your future development needs. During your performances, you will be continually seeking to improve your performance and it is imperative that you always think ahead about the impact that this will have on your future performances.

The previous table considers possible future development needs, based on the evidence gathered from monitoring.

Activity 9.3

Consider the types of evidence you have gathered from your monitoring and evaluating. What impact does this have on a factor(s)? What needs to happen in the future?

An example has been given. Use the table to think about your personal future development needs. Remember to take this from the evidence you have gathered in your monitoring and evaluating.

Evidence	Factor and impact	Future development need
From my training diary statements, I have noted that my anxiety levels before a performance have decreased, allowing me to concentrate on my role and my responsibilities more effectively. However my decisions are still not made promptly and this can have an impact on my anxiety.	Mental and emotional. Although my anxiety levels have decreased, I still do not take action quickly enough. I feel I have a lot more focus, but my slow decision making means that I do not react in time to have a successful impact on my performance.	I need to continue to develop an approach to decrease my anxiety levels, especially when making important decisions during my performance. I will work on a 'positive outlook approach', both during my practices and performances.

Check your progress

This chapter has looked at the ways you can monitor and evaluate performance. Answer the following questions to check whether you have a sound understanding of the key principles.

	HELP NEEDED	GETTING THERE	CONFIDENT
1. Explain why you need to monitor and evaluate performance.			

Advice from marker – Give reasons why the process of keeping check on the work you are doing will help you set new targets and also make sure it is having a positive impact on your performance.

	HELP NEEDED	GETTING THERE	CONFIDENT
2. Describe two methods to monitor and evaluate performance.			

Advice from marker – Give details about what the methods look like, what the protocol should be and how, when and where you would set these up.

	HELP NEEDED	GETTING THERE	CONFIDENT
3. Explain why these methods are appropriate.			

Advice from marker – give your reasons for using these methods. Convince the marker that if you were to do the same again that your methods were the best to use to get valid, accurate and reliable data before you begin training.

	HELP NEEDED	GETTING THERE	CONFIDENT
4. Evaluate your future development needs.			

Advice from marker – using the data (opinions, facts and figures) you have collected, explain what parts of your performance still give you problems and which bits you can now say (based on the evidence you have) require less attention. Try to be convincing about what you would be able to do if this new/future development need was improved.

Appendix: Sample programme of work to develop performance

Name: Calum Duncan

Activity: Volleyball

Specific training priorities:

1. Improve height of jump for effective spiking and blocking (Physical factor – fitness).
2. Manage emotions when mistiming spikes (Emotional factor).
3. Improve anticipation to increase effectiveness of blocking (Mental factor).

Priority	Approach to be used	Number of sessions
Jump height	Plyometrics	2 sessions per week working on leg strength
Management of emotions	'Parking'	Every practice game and drill in training
Anticipation	Structured approach drills	Twice a week as part of team training

Plan for a typical week:

	Plyometrics	Parking	Structured approach drills
Monday	*	*	
Tuesday		*	*
Wednesday	*	*	
Thursday		*	*
Friday	Rest	Rest	Rest
Saturday	GAME	*	GAME
Sunday	Rest	Rest	Rest

Diary entries for two days:

	Plyometrics	Parking	Structured approach drills
Monday	3 sets of zig zag hops, 3 sets of 6 depth jumps and 3 sets of lateral hurdle jumps with double rest times between sets.	As I go through the plyometric training, when I felt I was getting tired and angry at myself for not being able to complete the training without feeling pain, I used 'park it' making myself picture the end of the session, forcing myself to keep going, pushing myself to focus on completing the correct number of repetitions with quality. In the game at the end of the training session I used 'park it' again each time I made a poor block – even when my coach shouted at me.	
Tuesday		As we trained the new set plays, I made sure that as soon as one of the attempts was over I did not dwell on it if it was unsuccessful. I moved quickly on to the next attempt. As the session went on my timing and anticipation improved to the extent that when in the spiking position, I achieved 14 out of a possible 23 spikes to the target area and when in the game at the end, I felt more confident about blocking and spiking.	The drills the coach had set up were really to encourage the setters to be more creative. However, as this introduced some new 'set plays' for the team, I was able to watch the body language of our setters as they prepared to play long and reverse sets. This helped me practise the required run up to ensure I was arriving on time to hit the ball when it was at the correct height for an effective spike. This also helped my anticipation for blocking as I could see the slight difference in body position of our setter when he was going to reverse set. This gave me a little extra second to adjust and go to the correct place to block. I managed 4 out of 6 possible blocks successfully.

Here is another example of a training regime for a trampolinist.

Name: Megan McLean

Activity: Trampolining

Specific training priorities:

1. Improve LME in order to sustain height of bounce in last seconds of routine (Physical factor – fitness).
2. Manage performance development with no personal individual coach (Social factor).
3. Improve mental toughness when competing (Mental factor).

Priority	Approach to be used	Number of sessions
Jump height maintained	Circuits	3 sessions per week working on leg and core LME
Management of issues relating to working in isolation	'Support' approach	Every practice session
Mental toughness	'Reframing'	Twice a week as part of club training and at every competition

Plan for a typical week:

	Circuits	Support approach	Reframing
Monday	*	*	*
Tuesday			
Wednesday	*	*	*
Thursday			
Friday	*	*	*
Saturday			
Sunday	Competition	Competition	Competition

Diary entry:

	Circuits	Support approach	Reframing
Monday	8 station circuit 45 seconds at each station, repeated for 3 sets, time recorded to complete 18 mins 28 secs.	Remind myself of the routine, divert my attention away from other performers' performances and rehearse, carry out then evaluate own performance. Agree a time for 'debrief' from team coach who will confirm or correct my own evaluation of strengths and weaknesses and agree training priorities for next training session.	In training for back drop to front drop I told myself as I landed off centre on the bed coming out of my back drop that I would drive my hips up on the second attempt in order to gain a better position to go into my front drop.

001/15012015

10 9 8 7 6 5 4 3 2

ISBN 9780007549313

Published by
Leckie & Leckie Ltd
An imprint of HarperCollins*Publishers*
Westerhill Road, Bishopbriggs, Glasgow, G64 2QT
T: 0844 576 8126 F: 0844 576 8131
leckieandleckie@harpercollins.co.uk
www.leckieandleckie.co.uk

Publisher: Fiona Burns
Project manager: Craig Balfour

Special thanks to
Roda Morrison (copy edit)
Louise Robb (proofread)
Lauren Reid (image research)
Jouve (layout)

The Publishers would like to thank Robin Leckie, Jill Paterson, Donna Spence and Colin Steven of Airdrie Academy for their assistance with this publication.

Printed in Italy by Grafica Veneta S.P.A.

A CIP Catalogue record for this book is available from the British Library.

Acknowledgements

SCAT Test on page 50 from Martens, R. et al. (1990) Competitive Anxiety in Sport. Leeds: Human Kinetics.

Information on the 6 Cs types of communication on page 136 from Crookes (1991) Complan Column. Athletics Coach, 25 (3), p. 1.

PaceTracker app images on P63 © PaceTracker

P2 tennis - ©Lucy Clark / Shutterstock.com; P3 Germany World Cup team - ©Jefferson Bernardes / Shutterstock.com; P3 Andy Murray - ©lev radin / Shutterstock.com; P14–15 ©Robert Cianflone / Staff / Getty Images; P18 ©Ian MacNicol / Contributor / Getty Images; P19 Volleyball - © muzsy / Shutterstock.com; P21 injury - ©Tumar / Shutterstock.com; P21 Football - © Natursports / Shutterstock.com; P22 © Cameron Spencer / Staff / Getty Images; P23 Football - © Mark Runnacles / Stringer / Getty Images; P23 tennis - © Clive Brunskill / Staff / Getty Images; P24 © Jefferson Bernardes / Shutterstock.com; P25 © CARL COURT / Stringer / Getty Images; P26 © Gabriel Rossi/STF / Contributor / Getty Images; P32 © Neale Cousland / Shutterstock.com; P33 Usain Bolt - © Alexander Hassenstein / Staff / Getty Images; P33 gymnast © Julian Finney / Staff / Getty Images; P34 basketball - © Natursports / Shutterstock.com; P34 Jessica Ennis-Hill - © Harry Engels / Stringer / Getty Images; P35 Rory McIlroy © David W. Leindecker / Shutterstock.com; P35 netball - © Sean Garnsworthy / Staff / Getty Images; P36 athlete - © Maxisport / Shutterstock.com; P36 GOLFER - © photogolfer / Shutterstock.com; p36 Lionel Messi - © Natursports / Shutterstock.com; P37 trampoline - © Ronald Martinez / Staff / Getty Images; P37 hockey - © EcoPrint / Shutterstock.com; P38 volleyball - © Jamie Roach / Shutterstock.com; P38 football - © Lario Tus / Shutterstock.com; P40–41 © Richard Heathcote / Staff / Getty Images; P45 Ronaldo - © Anadolu Agency / Contributor / Getty Images; P45 Andy Murray - © ANDREW COWIE / Stringer / Getty Images; P45 swimmer - © Bob Thomas / Contributor / Getty Images; P46 © muzsy / Shutterstock.com; P49 Usain Bolt - © FRANCK FIFE / Staff / Getty Images; P49 Tom Daley - © Boris Streubel / Stringer / Getty Images; P52 Zidane - © AFP / Stringer / Getty Images; P52 red card - © muzsy / Shutterstock.com; P55 Rooney/Van Persie - melis / Shutterstock.com; P55 Barcelona - © Maxisport / Shutterstock.com; P56 © Aspen Photo/ shutterstock.com; P59 © Aspen Photo / Shutterstock.com; P60 © Andy Lidstone / Shutterstock.com; P61 © Aspen Photo / Shutterstock.com; P65 © Maxisport/shutterstock.com; P67 © Mitch Gunn/shutterstock.com; P71 © muzsy/shutterstock.com; P72 gymnast - © Clive Rose / Staff; P72 football - © Pool / Pool / Getty Images; P72 tennis - © lev radin / Shutterstock.com; P73 © Dmitry Morgan / Shutterstock.com; P74 © Jeff J Mitchell / Staff/ Getty Images; P75 © Rnoid / Shutterstock.com; P76 Messi/De Jong - © AGIF / Shutterstock.com; P76 Mourinho - © mooinblack / Shutterstock.com; P76 red card - © Dan Mullan / Stringer / Getty Images; P77 hockey - © EcoPrint / Shutterstock.com; P82–83 © Alex Livesey / Staff /Getty Images; P84 © Dave J Hogan / Contributor / Getty Images; P85 © AFP / Stringer / Getty Images; P86 © FlashStudio / Shutterstock.com; P88 Messi - © AGIF / Shutterstock.com; P89 © Stefan Holm / Shutterstock.com; P90 © rolfo/Getty Images; P91 © emran/shutterstock.com; P92 © Paolo Bona/shutterstock.com ; P92 © Rena Schild / Shutterstock.com; P93© Aspen Photo/shutterstock.com; P94 Jamie Roach/shutterstock.com, "MalawiFijiNetball" by Grant Williamson - Own work/wikicommons, Pavel L Photo and Video/shutterstock.com, Denis Kuvaev/shutterstock.com, CHEN WS/ shutterstock.com, wavebreakmedia/shutterstock.com; P96 © muzsy / Shutterstock.com; P97 © Pal2iyawit / Shutterstock.com; P97 © Lilyana Vynogradova/shutterstock.com; P101 © THOMAS COEX / Staff / Getty Images; P103 © Getty Images; p104 © Gustavo Fadel / Shutterstock.com; P106 © Maxisport / Shutterstock.com; P107 © Natursports / Shutterstock.com; P109 © Aspen Photo / Shutterstock.com; P111 © Chris Hellyar / Shutterstock.com; P112 © Mai Techaphan / Shutterstock.com; P117 © Herbert Kratky / Shutterstock.com; P125 © Matt Trommer / Shutterstock.com; P129 © mooinblack / Shutterstock.com; P130 ANDRE DURAO/shutterstock.com; bikeriderlondon/shutterstock.com; P130 © David Cannon / Staff / Getty Images; P130 © Clive Brunskill / Staff / Getty Images; P131 © Paolo Bona/shutterstock.com; P131 © AGIF / Shutterstock.com; P131 © Clive Rose / Staff; P132 © thelefty / Shutterstock.com; P136 © Jamie Roach / Shutterstock.com; P136 © Maxisport / Shutterstock.com; P137 © PAUL ELLIS / Staff / Getty Images; P137 © Matt Trommer / Shutterstock.com; P138 © Jamie Roach / Shutterstock.com; P140 © Mitch Gunn / Shutterstock.com; P141 © Andrey Yurlov / Shutterstock.com ; P142 © Washington Post/ Getty Images; P143 © Ben Blankenburg / Getty Images; P144–146 © Robin Leckie; P147 © CHEN WS / Shutterstock.com; P147 © David W. Leindecker / Shutterstock.com; P147© muzsy / Shutterstock.com; P149 © Neale Cousland / Shutterstock.com; P149 © Suhaimi Abdullah / Stringer / Getty Images; P149 © Natursports / Shutterstock.com; P150 © Paolo Bona / Shutterstock.com; P150 © muzsy / Shutterstock.com; P152 © anantachat / Shutterstock.com; P154 © AGIF / Shutterstock.com; P154 © karnizz / Shutterstock.com; P155 © Paolo Bona / Shutterstock.com; P156 © Marcos Mesa Sam Wordley / Shutterstock.com; P157 © Anton Gvozdikov / Shutterstock.com; P159 © Corepics VOF / Shutterstock.com; P159 © Ivica Drusany / Shutterstock.com; P161 © Sergey Petrov / Shutterstock.com, AGIF / Shutterstock.com, Aspen Photo / Shutterstock.com; AHMAD FAIZAL YAHYA / Shutterstock.com , shutterstock.com, luca85 / Shutterstock.com; P163 © almonfoto / Shutterstock.com; P163 © Denis Kuvaev / Shutterstock.com; P166 © Natursports / Shutterstock.com; P167 © photofriday / Shutterstock.com; P169 © ROBERTO ZILLI / Shutterstock.com; P170 © Herbert Kratky / Shutterstock.com; P170 © Cameron Spencer / Staff / Getty Images; P171 © Denis Kuvaev / Shutterstock.com; P172 © Jamie McDonald / Staff / Getty Images; P172 © Andy Lyons / Staff; P174 © AFP/Getty Images; P174 © Sporting News via Getty Images; P175 © Natursports / Shutterstock.com; Inge Schepers / Shutterstock.com; P182–183 © ADRIAN DENNIS / Staff / Getty Images